WOW! 2

The memoirito continues....

By David Pérez
Author of WOW!

ISBN 978-09862706-80

Cover & Interior Design: SpicerDigital

Printed in USA

An early version of chapter one, titled "Dean of Discipline,"
appeared in the December 2011 issue of the online journal
Somos en Escrito.

Selections from the U.S. Navy chapters were read on
October 2015 at Lenny Foster's Living Light Gallery in Taos,
New Mexico in an event organized by the *Taos Journal of
International Poetry & Art.*

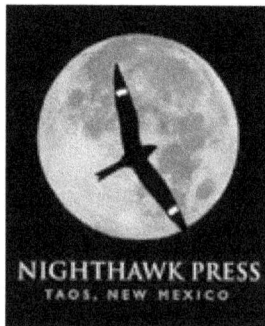

NIGHTHAWK PRESS
TAOS, NEW MEXICO

www.nighthawkpress.com

To Veronica, for all love

To Milton Vera, for changing my life
Rest in peace, my brother

Acknowledgements

This book has gone through so many renderings in its five-year journey to publication, that it's difficult to remember all the people who gave me wonderful encouragement and feedback along the way. So please forgive me if I leave you out. Whatever your help entailed, thank you so much!

That said, there are people I recall well who guided me through this process and provided much-needed direction and skills. Thanks to Connie Josefs for your work on an early version of my Navy chapter. For various moments of inspiration and connecting with my roots, thank you Harold, Linda, Rosie, Edgar, and Enrique.

Thank you family: Jase Miles-Perez and Jelayne Miles for thoughtful comments on early versions of the manuscript. A double thanks to my son Jase for giving the book a final reading and offering invaluable advice.

Thank you to my daughter Belinda Maria for all that you do. Thank you to my brother George for the sharing of a young life. Thank you to my parents Jorge Perez and Luz Maria Izquierdo for always being there, now and forever.

Thank you to the Milton Vera family for letting me share memories about Milton after he passed away. Thank you Raphael Ramos for being part of so much of my life; hope you're doing well in the great beyond. Thank you Danny Rivera for being my brother in so many ways. Thank you Workers World Party for providing the nexus of my life's direction at just the right time.

Thank you Mandala Center and Opus House for giving me space to write. Thank you Wired? Café, where I spent many a day working on my book. Thank you Taos for providing endless manna for inspiration.

Thank you South Bronx and the Millbrook Houses!

Gracias Teresita Dovalpage for pushing my writing forward. Thank you Jan Smith for your continuing advice and for our work together. And SOMOS, the Literary Heart of Taos, for the many ways you help writers.

A grand thanks to Barb Scott of Final Eyes for spot-on copy-editing and proofreading expertise. Thank you Sydney Morgan (Fiverr) for a final round of proofreading.

Thank you Jeff Spicer of SpicerDigital for the stellar book cover and interior design services. Thank you Rebecca Lenzini and Nighthawk Press for publishing my book!

And a zillion thanks to Veronica Golos: wife, poet, teacher, biggest fan, honest editor, and eternal source of love.

CHAPTER ONE

On the first day of high school the bell rings, signaling the end of Freshman Orientation Day at Cardinal Hayes Memorial High School for Boys. My backpack is laden with enough textbooks and spiral binders to cause spinal spasms. So I'm both weighed down and sweaty when I exit the school into the early September heat, thermometer already at 90 degrees, humidity just as high. A New York City heat.

I take off my blazer, loosen my tie, and begin the two-block walk down Grand Concourse to the 149th Street subway station. A voice cries out, "Hey you!" It's Father McCormick, the school's six-foot-three Dean of Discipline. I scamper over.

"Yes, Father?"

"What do you think you're doing, son?"

"When?"

"Not when; what."

"What what?"

"Don't get funny on me, young man!"

"I wasn't—"

"You're supposed to keep your jacket on until you arrive at the subway. Didn't you hear me explain the rules in the auditorium?"

I did but figured he was joking. *Keep our jackets on for two blocks?*

"Come inside to my office," he says.

"Can I leave my jacket off?"

He ignores me. I put the blue blazer back on and straighten my tie. *God, it's freaking hot.*

Father McCormick sits me down in his manicured lair, located in the first office on the left when you enter the school. The door is solid mahogany with a brass doorknob. "What's your name, son?"

"David Perez," I answer, putting the accent on the last syllable of my last name. For some reason, a lot of folks, including many of my friends, were pronouncing it that way. But the accent really goes on the first syllable. It would be decades before I consciously made the effort to say my family name correctly.

"Mr. Perez, you must think we're playing games here," he says, parking his tall frame on the edge of an impressively simonized desk.

"Not really."

"The rules we have at Hayes are for a reason. Strong rules make for good, strong boys. Does that make sense?"

"Sounds reasonable."

"So is this."

Father McCormick passes me a chit stamped "After School Detention," also known as JUG, derived from the Latin *jugum*, meaning yoke or burden. My fellow students would come to call JUG, *Justice Under God.*

"What class are you in, son?"

"1M. Honors," I say.

"Not a good way to start off, is it?"

"Could be worse."

The Dean of Discipline smiles cryptically. "You're funny. I don't like funny."

***

Detention entails standing in a classroom for forty minutes while reading a book, or simply standing. I choose the latter. Four other students are there, all white. I should say seem white because Puerto Ricans come in a rainbow of skin colors and facial features. We could be as dark-skinned as a *moreno* or fair-skinned with red hair and freckles, like my buddy Melvin, aka Colorao. Nonetheless, these guys look white, as in *blanquito*. Call it body language, aura, whatever. You could just tell.

The teacher in the room yawns. I do the same. I feel great being in detention, actually, like it proves that I'm somehow still a badass despite being an honors student. Which is kind of silly, I know. I've always had this duality: being smart in school while also getting into trouble. The thing is, just like my getting detention for taking off a stupid jacket, I tend to land in trouble mostly for stupid shit.

Like at St. Luke's, the South Bronx neighborhood school on 139th Street near Cypress Avenue, where I'd graduated from three months earlier, in June 1969. I'd been an altar boy at St.

Luke's Church for two years and ended up getting canned for "The Baby Jesus Fiasco," when my dim buddy Julio accidentally broke Baby Jesus' foot right before Christmas Midnight Mass and I hurriedly but unsuccessfully tried to cover up the damage with Scotch tape, leaving the severed foot dangling for all the priests to see. Furious over the "desecration," they banished Julio and me from the Altar Boy Society, which meant I could no longer gaze longingly at girls' tongues when they received Holy Communion, the reason I'd become an altar boy in the first place.

Then there was "The Church Attic Debacle," which almost got me expelled from school altogether. A month before graduation, a group of us snuck into the church attic, hoping to find hidden treasure: something we could pawn, like priceless goblets. Instead, we encountered thick dust, broken furniture, and inexplicably discarded silverware.

"Hey guys, check this out," Julio whispered. He was kneeling over slats on the floor, which you could see through to the church below. Then he spat, right down on Father Kelly, walking down the center aisle. The spit barely missed him. He looked up. Busted.

Later, in the church office, a livid Father Kelly insisted on expelling us for the mortal sin of "transgression against church property."

"Is that one of the Ten Commandments?" I asked.

"Shut up."

Fortunately, the newly installed pastor, Father Ryan, who wore beads and a black beret, overruled our threatened expulsion.

"Telling your parents will be punishment enough," he said.

"Amen," chimed Julio.

"Shut up," said a disappointed Father Kelly.

I was grounded for two weeks. My mother felt that what I had done was bad, but certainly no violation of the Holy Canon. Pops didn't care one way or the other. He left all things relating to church and school in Mami's hands. But he was curious.

"Why you go to the basement?"

"It was the attic, Pops."

"They're all stupid."

Pops has a habit of speaking in non-sequiturs, and it's useless getting him to stay on point. But he was right. It was stupid, all of it.

And there I was at Cardinal Hayes, keeping tradition alive. Another school bell rang.

Detention ended. The teacher got up and stretched. I hauled up my backpack. A part of me shrugged it off as if I'd easily performed hard labor. I also wondered if this whole detention thing was a warning to watch my step. I'd come to Cardinal Hayes on a mission, one that had nothing to do with stupid shit.

CHAPTER TWO

Before graduating from St. Luke's Junior High School, I'd taken the Specialized High School Admissions Test to see if I could get into Stuyvesant or the Bronx High School of Science, the crème de la crème of public high schools in New York City. The SHSAT had taken place at Bronx Science, which was my top choice.

Arriving at the school, at 205th Street between Goulden and Paul Avenues in the north Bronx, all I could mutter was, "Wow." Hundreds of kids roamed the rolling grounds, gawking at the spread of buildings that housed a mathematics lab, a sophisticated IBM computer, a planetarium, a radio station, two greenhouses, an animal room, six advanced-science labs for group work, and three labs for individual student research. The huge school bordered the equally sprawling Lehman College campus and the Jerome Park Reservoir, built in 1906 to serve the Croton Aqueduct as part of New York City's water-supply system.

"This is like another planet!" a nerdy white kid exclaimed to no one in particular. He had eighty pens in his shirt pocket.

"Far out," added a Grateful Dead type with torn jeans and long hair. I was surprised to see hippies here. I figured them to be mostly anti-learning and anti-hard work. Then again, they might have thought the same about me, a Puerto Rican wearing sharkskin pants and white converse sneakers, the Latino fashion statement of the times.

Speaking of 'Ricans, there weren't too many of us there. As I mentioned before, my internal radar could usually tell when someone was a *blanquito*, and Bronx Science was swarming with them—a mass gathering of the heavily blond. Blacks were equally scarce. Some wore Dashikis and looked as hip as I did. Others looked as dorky as the white kids in high-water pants and thick glasses.

I took a deep breath. I hadn't studied for the SHSAT, nor had any of my teachers urged me to. They were like, "Good luck, David!" and that was that. But I had strong academic chops, no question about that. Starting in the third grade at Public School 65, where I scored an excellent in every category, including "Personal Hygiene," and on through my transfer to St. Luke's, where every report card came filled with 90s and A's, I had consistently been in the top of my class.

But this was a whole other universe, populated by hundreds of fellow brainiacs. I asked myself: *Do I really belong here?*

When I entered the main lobby, a 63-foot mural of noted scientists greeted me. According to the school brochure, the Venetian-glass mosaic painting, completed in 1959, served to remind students, staff, and visitors of the "paramount importance of the life of the mind." I sagely nodded my head in agreement.

The SHSAT was hard, as in goddamn hard. There weren't

any science questions, thank God, but the math was maddening, especially the multiple-choice questions, where each possible answer was separated by one digit. Then came the evil sentence math. I'm sure you're familiar with it: If Sally weighed 90 pounds, and Bill weighed 120 pounds, then how tall was Sam? Or the equally diabolical: If a plane left the Chicago airport at 11 a.m. traveling at 300 miles an hour, and another plane left Moscow the day before, traveling at the speed of sound, how long then before they blah, blah—who gave a flying shit? A clock on the wall counted the minutes as I circled my best guesses with a No. 2 pencil.

I was on more solid ground with the reading/writing section. At least I understood the questions, knew about content, reasoning and grammar. Still, by the time I was three-quarters of the way through, my brain shifted into lockdown. I began rapidly filling in blanks at random, pretending I was breezing through the material. I handed the test to the instructor.

"Piece of cake," I crowed.

***

A few days later, I took the Catholic High School Entrance Exam. Mami preferred I continue with a Catholic-school education, but supported and understood my shooting for the elite public schools. Pops' reigning motto, spoken with beer can in hand, was, "Go the right way, and you'll never go the wrong way."

This time around, I studied. The test turned out to be far

easier than the SHSAT, albeit still sprinkled with those un-
nerving sentence math problems. Oh, and also graphs, which
for some reason always got me flustered. To this day, whenever
I read, "As this graph clearly shows..." I enter mental-block land.
Sorry, the graph doesn't clearly show anything. Nevertheless, I
was confident that I did well.

Then the results arrived in the mail. As expected, I didn't
make the SHSAT cut, although I had hoped for a miracle, that
my mindless guessing had been uncannily accurate. At first, I
thought about bragging to my friends that I had *finally failed a
test*, that I had seen the light and stopped "giving a shit" about
stupid tests and stupid school. Being cool and being school
smart didn't go together living in the South Bronx, a law never
spoken but clearly understood. "Not giving a shit," on the other
hand, was a badge of honor, and that badge was worn openly.

But I kept the news to myself, mainly because I did give a
shit. Even while being defensive about it, I enjoyed doing well in
school. I was also competitive about it. At St. Luke's, other top
students and I vied for the quarterly Medal of Excellence, a little
gold pin adorned with the face of Jesus Christ. I got privately
pissed when I didn't win the award and made certain it rarely
happened.

The letter from the Catholic High School Entrance Exam
handed me another slice of humble pie. My first choice, Cardinal Spellman, considered the top academic Catholic high school

in New York City, rejected me. Blessedly, Cardinal Hayes, my second choice, said yes. I sighed in relief and forced myself to be pleased. George, my year-older brother, attended Hayes and liked it.

"It's a good school," George said after I told him the news. "The teachers aren't crazy, but they push you. They got a great athletic department. Not that I would notice."

We laughed. George wasn't big on sports, being self-admittedly somewhat of a klutz. Stickball, roller-skating, it didn't matter. He tried them, became frustrated and gave up. Despite being six inches taller and twenty pounds heavier than me, George wasn't athletic at all; his passion came from writing and drawing comic books, including creating his own characters and storylines.

It was nice to know that the teachers at Hayes weren't loony, however. At St. Luke's, George and I had survived the reign of the Brothers of the Sacred Heart. And let me tell you, there wasn't anything sacred about them. The Brothers' arsenal ranged from paddles the size of two-by-fours to slaps to the face. My seventh-grade warden, Brother Lawrence, went into such fits of rage that he twice went up and down the aisle hitting *everyone* in the class with his splintered paddle, smacking each of us on the back, between the shoulder blades.

"You're right, George, I should be happy."

"You should. So stop being all mopey."

I smiled, but inside I was reliving the exams. I gave myself excuses: I was overconfident. I hadn't studied. I hadn't studied enough. I wasn't prepared. Only the last excuse rang true, but in a confusing way, a kind of wondering: *Why* wasn't I prepared?

When I realized the reason decades later, it saddened me with its stark simplicity. I wasn't prepared because my school simply had not, and could not, prepare me. Not from neglect, mind you, nor because of uncaring teachers. Despite laying it on extra thick with corporal punishment, my teachers did care about their students, did want us to succeed. And St. Luke's was a good school compared to Public School 65, which I had attended until third grade. But PS 65 was already on its way to becoming the worst-performing elementary school in New York City, immortalized years later in educator and author Jonathan Kozol's 1995 bestseller, *Amazing Grace: The Trials and Tribulations of Everyday Life*, which details the apartheid-like conditions in what had become the poorest congressional district in the United States.

So compared to PS 65, St. Luke's was better and more challenging. But it was still a school in the South Bronx, where the odds were stacked heavily against success. Notwithstanding all this, I knew in my bones that I had solid academic chops. I did belong up there with la crème. When I began freshman year at Cardinal Hayes Memorial High School for Boys, I vowed never to be unprepared and overconfident again.

CHAPTER THREE

The day after detention, I hunkered down and got busy. I had scored high enough in the Catholic School Entrance Exam to make the Hayes Honors Class: Homeroom 1M. Of the thirty-five or so classmates, about a dozen were Black and Latino. It was my first official class as a "minority." To my surprise, I didn't feel out of place. In fact, it felt remarkably unremarkable, a kind of, hey, this is just how is it. Moreover, I discovered that I actually liked the toothy white nerds in class: their bottled glasses, their love of playing spitball, their corny "Joke of the Day!"

It would take years for me to define it, but I was learning about a kind of dual racial consciousness in my character. One aspect of me nursed a strong pride in being Puerto Rican, in being our people, a color and nation specificity, even with Latinos coming in a rainbow of colors and being from different nations. Another part of me, unbeknownst until my time in Hayes, held an equally strong pride in belonging anywhere and everywhere, a color and nation blindness if you will, comfortable in diversity with all its layers and weirdness. Again, I couldn't name this identity duality at the time, being only fourteen. But there it was, unfolding in classroom 1M.

My class schedule included physics, taught by Mr. Montagino, a teacher whose enthusiasm was contagious—"See that liquid bubbling? It's a bunch of excited electrons!"— and I finally related to science beyond the wonders of comic books. Say what you will about the comic genre, but that's where you'll find stories teeming with physics: electrically charged cosmos, parallel universes, and laboratory experiments galore. Mr. Montagino smiled when I said he reminded me of the mystical comic-book character Dr. Strange. "I read him too!" he exclaimed.

Algebra was another pleasant surprise, with its world of formulas and x's and y's. I took to it easily. Perhaps that was due to Mr. Delaney, another great teacher who was also my homeroom advisor. One thing Cardinal Hayes had in spades was quality faculty.

Not surprisingly, I have no memories of religion class, most likely my response to yet more rote teaching. Either that or I already knew enough to zone things out. At St. Luke's, I had completed my Sacraments and was aware of what it took to enter Heaven: namely being without sin, or at the very least being truly sorry about committing them. I had been an altar boy and attended Mass every Sunday. What else did I need to know? Anyway, I aced religion too.

Ironically, the only class I struggled with was "Spanish I Special," also called Spanish II. Being that I was Puerto Rican, the school assumed—no one asked me—that I knew the language well enough for a level-two course. If only. The last time I spoke only Spanish was at the age of two when I tugged on

my mother's apron and exclaimed that I'd learned my first English word: wow. After that, with my parents' encouragement,
my brother, George and I rapidly learned English by reading
comic books aloud and watching endless television. By the age
of ten, I was English dominant, and I had forgotten a lot of
Spanish, which wasn't too much of a problem because many of
my friends suffered the same fate. We were part of the nascent
Nuyorican population, the first generation of Puerto Ricans
born and raised in New York City, a coming-of-age defined by
continuity and transformation. Our new language, Spanglish,
hybridized the two languages and also hatched new words, like
roofo for roof instead of *techo*. Nuyorican culture would play a
pivotal role in the development of rap, hip-hop and slam poetry.

Becoming less fluent in Spanish was more of a problem
when I visited my legions of aunts, uncles, and cousins in
Caguas, Puerto Rico, a lusciously green country hamlet where
both my parents were born and raised. I went there with my
folks about twice a year, and invariably I would feel embarrassed
over the loss of my native tongue, fielding my relatives' blank
stares whenever I lapsed into grammatical mistakes, which was
often. They were kind about it, though. Understanding. Mostly.
Sometimes.

At Cardinal Hayes, my lack of fluency and ill grammar
played out terribly in Spanish II, mainly because the class was
taught entirely in Spanish, so half the time I had no idea what

our teacher, Brother Rueda (*de España!*) was talking about. Plus he had an annoying habit of tossing us candy (*un caramelo!*) whenever we got an answer right, as if we were trained seals. Still, Brother Rueda was a welcome change from the nutcase Brothers of the Sacred Heart. Give me a *caramelo* over a paddle any day.

***

At St. Luke's, I had been the school's top sprinter, winning dozens of gold medals at events sponsored by either some Catholic-school association or the Police Athletic League. I was eager to start running for the Hayes track-and-field team, but decided to first try out for the freshmen football squad as a wide receiver. In the playgrounds and large lawns of the Millbrook Houses, I'd played innumerable games of two-hand touch and tackle football, and acquired an ego-boosting reputation as crazy fucker who never wore a helmet when tackling thundering dudes like Fat Ray and Gorilla.

Hayes had a good-sized sports field in the back of the main building, and the tryouts were crowded with prospective head bangers. The coach was duly impressed with how I protectively cradled the ball after catching it, so as not to fumble. Running patterns like a buttonhook and slant were familiar, and whenever the quarterback said "Go deep," I outraced the defender into the end zone.

"I like your speed and hands, David!" the coach said. "But

you need to put some meat on your bones. What are you, 120 pounds?"

"One fifteen."

"Five foot eight?"

"Five foot seven."

"You have to fatten up."

"What about getting taller?"

Since I didn't really want to gain weight—and I couldn't gain height—I opted not to attend the next round of tryouts, and just as well. At Cardinal Hayes, they took their football seriously. Some of the guys vying for the squad clocked in at 250-plus pounds: brick houses with crew cuts, snarling and drooling to mete out concussions. If these behemoths were at Hayes, they'd certainly have counterparts at opposing schools, animals eager to give brain damage to bony wide receivers like me, even with a padded helmet. Was this how I wanted to spend my Sundays?

I stuck to track-and-field. The coach, Mr. Slater, a pleasant chap with a face shaped like the Joker, marked me as "a fast sprinter with tremendous promise." Even as I specialized in the 100- and 200-yard dashes, at Hayes everyone had to compete in everything, and that included running cross-country, a two-mile trek through a rock-strewn trail in Van Cortland Park in the north Bronx. I had first tried cross-country in St. Mary's Park as part of our athletic conditioning at St. Luke's. Brother

Lawrence was the school's sports coach, mainly because he carried a clipboard and knew how to blow a whistle. He reveled in seeing our seventh-grade class wheeze up and down the steepest concrete paths of the park. I always gasped when I reached the finish line. The chain smokers had it worst.

At Hayes, I discovered that with a knowledgeable coach—Mr. Slater himself was a runner—I could push myself more than I thought possible. One brisk October day, I placed in the top ten of a cross-country meet, Mr. Slater urging me on, yelling, "You're beautiful!" as I found my second wind. It was my most profound experience with the kick, the latent reservoir of extra energy that allows a runner to pour it on in the last part of the race, saving their best for last, actually gaining momentum as they reach the tape. I'd experienced the kick before, but never at that depth, never when I felt at the edge of collapse.

After the race, Coach Slater asked, "How did that feel?"

"Amazing. Wow. I thought I was done."

He smiled. "Finding that extra kick is always special, David. And it's always there, waiting for you. You remember that, okay?"

CHAPTER FOUR

Digging deep served me on the academic front as well. On October 26, 1969, at the end of the school day, I received my report card for the first marking period.

If you squint, you can see that out of 714 students, I ranked 003, Number 3. And if it weren't for the 86 I scored in Spanish, I likely would have ranked Number One, *Numero Uno*. I had expected the report card to be excellent, but hadn't dreamed it would be so momentous.

When I went to my locker, guys in the hall were pointing and whispering: "That's the guy who..." and "On the track team, he's also..." I put away my textbooks, spun the combination lock with a flourish, and marveled on how fast news traveled.

There's a scene near the end of a *Star Trek* episode called "Balance of Terror," when Captain Kirk walks down the corridors of the Starship Enterprise after defeating an enemy Romulan ship armed with a cloaking device. As the credits roll, the camera lingers on Kirk's walk: confident, proud. That's exactly how I felt strutting down the corridors at Cardinal Hayes Memorial School for Boys: Captain Kirk with a ditty-bop, dressed in sharkskin pants and Playboy shoes, confident and proud. I was not only school smart, but also street smart—and I reminded my classmates of that fact whenever I could. Yeah, I exaggerated, made myself this tough hombre from "Killer's Land," as I called my South Bronx neighborhood. But I *did* know the streets, even if magnified in my imagination.

Near the school exit, I ran into Father McCormick.

"Hi Father," I said.

"I remember you. The jacket I think it was. Well, congratulations."

"What?"

"I heard the news."

"You too? How?"

For the first time I heard Father McCormick laugh, a deep, rich rumble.

"God works in mysterious ways, son."

***

At home, my mother was thrilled.

"*¡Aye, que hijo inteligente yo tengo!*"

"Thanks Mami."

"*Ahora tiene que practicar su español.*"

"*Yo sé.* This way I can be number one. I mean, *esta manera que puedo ser número uno.*"

"That's right."

She promised to share the great news with my father when he got home.

"Whenever that is, *mijo*."

Mami had stopped lying about Pops being "with friends." She knew I knew the deal. Pops' "friends" were named Rheingold and Don Q, bosom buddies of poker and playing numbers. When the drinking and gambling combo resulted in winnings, however, Mami temporarily forgave Pops his trespasses, and purchased a new piece of furniture for our three-bedroom apartment. We lived at 165 St. Ann's Avenue in the Millbrook Houses, the public-housing projects in the Mott Haven section of South Bronx that ran from 135th Street to 137th Street, from Cypress Avenue to the east to Brook Avenue to the west. We used to live in another building, 600 East 137th Street, but moved to 165 when my brother and I became teenagers and wanted our own bedrooms.

When my family moved there in 1958, the Millbrook Houses were sparkling new, a virtual mini-city with crisp lawns, a humongous laundry, a well-attended daycare center, and a community center equipped with pool tables, Ping-Pong tables, and various after-school activities and sports leagues. Along with the Melrose and Port Morris sections, Mott Haven was part of what would later be designated Bronx Community District No. 1, the area with the highest concentration of housing projects in the Bronx—eleven complexes totaling 11,149 units.

Mami kissed me and went off to cook *bacalao guisado*, salted codfish stew, a favorite dish. I knocked on George's bedroom door.

"Enter, mutant," he said.

As he did most days, George was working on a new comic-book idea. Today, it was "The Terror Train." The main character looked like a cross between George and Elvis Presley.

"Those are some wicked sideburns," I said.

"Yes, and he'll soon discover *the true meaning of terror!* By the way, I heard the news already."

"You too? Are there like hidden microphones somewhere?"

"Maybe. Anyway, way to go little bro!"

"How did you do?"

"Okay I guess: a couple of 90s, a few 80s. No complaints. But this is about you, Dave. Your friends are going to pee in their pants when they hear the news."

"Um, I don't plan to tell them."

"Why the heck not?"

"I just don't like to talk about school with them. We talk about other stuff. You know, girls and sports and whatnot."

"You *never* talk about school with them? I don't believe that for a sec."

George was technically right. Chino, Julio and I did talk about school, except it was mainly about *their* schools, and education had very little to do with it.

Whenever I connected with my friends—usually on Sundays in the Big Park following a quick hello and fashion check at St. Luke's Church during morning Mass—they regaled me with tales of bendable rules and negligible homework. As for life on the block, it was all about smoking Chiba, a potent brand of marijuana dealt from the back door of our neighborhood pet shop. Occasionally Julio or Chino would ask, "So how's Hayes for horses?" I'd shrug and say, "It's okay." Then we'd move on to their lives.

"Look, George, I just don't want to show off. It's not important anyway."

"What are you talking about? They're your closest friends. That's what you always call them."

"They still are."

"Then what's the problem? I don't—"

"It's not a problem. You're the one making it a goddamn problem. Let it go!"

My brother sighed and continued to work on a Terror Train panel, penciling in a word balloon with "Aaarghh!"

I went into my room and closed the door. Taking after my mother, I kept my room neat: shoes and sneakers evenly lined up, clothes in the closet, no dust. I plopped onto my bed and simmered. George was right, and I knew it. How could I not share the news with guys like Chino and Julio? I mean, the whole neighborhood should know about this! I should be singing it from the fire escapes like Tony in *West Side Story*.

But I couldn't. And I didn't. For the first time in my young life, I had effectively separated life in school from life in the block. In elementary and middle school, the guys in school were the same guys I hung out with afterward in the playgrounds. That ended when we graduated from St. Luke's. In fact, the main reason I'd been able to achieve what I had was by limiting time with my friends. Each conversation ended more or less the same:

"You don't know what you're missing, Dave."

"Maybe one day, fellas."

"When?"

"Soon." Then I would race home to study. Before soon became now.

I got out of bed and stared out the window. Night was falling and the Bruckner Expressway was light with traffic. Looking southeast, I saw Queens. To my right was the Willis Avenue Bridge leading to Manhattan. It was a crossroads where I lived: the Mott Haven section of the South Bronx, as south in the neighborhood as you could get before you ended up in the Harlem River. It was tough and getting tougher. But it was home.

I got a revelation: Why not add just a little more time in the block? A beer here, a cigarette there, I mean, what's the big deal? Where's the harm? At the same time, I would continue to work hard in school because, hey, I still loved the learning zone I was in, still loved the ditty-bop in my step whenever I walked the corridors at Hayes. So what if my neighborhood buddies didn't know of my achievements? I knew, and that's all that mattered.

Mami knocked on door. "*Es hora de comer,*" she said.

George and I went to the dining table to eat, the smell of *bacalao guisado* filling the air like incense. The ubiquitous painting of the Last Supper hung on the wall, overseeing our meal. Next to the dining table were built-in shelves with family photos and Mami's porcelain figurines, her private art museum.

"Thanks, Mami," we said in unison.

"Thank my two smart boys," Mami said.

CHAPTER FIVE

ot long after, I was hugging a quart of Colt 45 with Chino. There were a lot of Chinos and Chinas in my neighborhood, reflecting the Asiatic features of Puerto Rico's Taíno Indian ancestors, the original inhabitants of the island then called Borinquen. Chino was an endearing label, much like Negro and Negrita. Often these became the only names you were known by.

This particular Chino, a friend of many years, was still boxing for the St. Mary's Recreational Club, but had pulled back on his training. Today he was on a roll about hooky gigs, daytime parties you went to by cutting class.

"Yo, Dave. I'm telling you, man, you get to do the 500 and grind and the *jebas* are like aye *pápi* and I'm like, damn, shit!"

"You're sweating, Chino."

"You would too if you was there."

"Where's there?"

"Basements. You know, places dark."

"Sounds spooky."

"You gotta party more, Dave."

"I party plenty!"

Well, not plenty. But I did party. After my first date with Linda Ramos two years earlier, where I danced like a klutz and couldn't muster up the courage to kiss her goodnight, I had finally boned up on my dancing and schemed out with a few girls, including a *jeba* at a school dance in the Hayes gymnasium. Her name was Sylvia, a Colombian chick from Cathedral, an all-girl's high school in downtown Manhattan.

After doing the 500 grind to the R&B ballad *Going in Circles*, Sylvia and I snuck into the boys' locker room and slobbered like maniacs. Sylvia had an endless well of saliva. At one point, I felt spit streaming down my chin.

"*Que rico tu eres*," my Latina spitfire said when we came up for air.

"*Rico como Puerto Rico*," I replied, exaggerating the trilled r's in a rather good imitation of Ricardo Montalbán. I wiped my chin and we tongue-kissed again. My erection pressed against her chiffon skirt. Sylvia pressed back, sweaty hand on my sweaty neck. Then, just like that, she backed away, smoothed out her miniskirt, and plopped a Life Saver into her mouth.

"I go now."

Before I could pant and beg, Sylvia turned and left the dance. I never saw her again.

Chino nudged me. "Come back, Dave."

"I was just remembering something."

"Sure."

"Like I said, Chino, I'm cool. You have your thing, I have mine."

"I dig mine better."

I dug his better too.

***

Fast-forward a month or so. This time, I was hanging out with Julio, newly coined Focus because of his oversized glasses. He was sitting on the stoop in front of his tenement building on 141st Street near Brook Avenue. Focus was thrilled to be attending Dodge Vocational High School, ostensibly to learn "business skills," which he claimed came in handy on Delancey Street, haggling with *judios* over the price of alpacas and sharkskin's. According to Focus, if you "got them business skills," you ended up with some fabulous deals. To wit:

Focus: "That's too much!"

Jewish shopkeeper: "But I make no money!"

Focus: "But I got no money!"

Jewish shopkeeper frowns: "Okay, I'll give you the pants for ten dollars."

Focus claps his hands: "Sold!"

When I sat down next to Focus, I admired his undoubtedly well-negotiated alpaca top and pepper-colored silk pants. But more than his clothes, I was drawn to his hair, which had grown to his shoulders. It framed his face perfectly, making his big round glasses look equally as hip as he did.

Focus noted my staring. "Hair looks good, right?

"You're doing it, man."

"So when are you doing it?"

I patted my short, wavy brown hair, slightly parted to the right side. "Gotta let the hair grow first."

"So grow your fucking hair."

"Can't. We got haircut inspections in school."

"You're shitting me."

I gave him the lowdown, how we lined up once a month in the gym while Father McCormack, our merry Dean of Discipline, played drill sergeant, walking up and down the ranks with a letter opener in his hand, looking for violations of the Hayes Hair Code. For straight hair like mine, his favorite method of uncovering a lawbreaker was to slide the letter opener under one side of the suspicious hair and, with a cheerful twist of his hairy wrist, flip it over to the parted side. If too much hair went over, you were told to go home immediately and return the following day with a "regulation" haircut, short and neat.

"And check this out," I continued. "With the Black guys, he dips the letter opener into their Afros. If it sinks in too deep, off to the barber you go."

"Heavy."

"It ain't too bad."

And I meant it. I liked Cardinal Hayes, despite the haircut inspections, despite the silly rules. It was a top-notch school with top-notch teachers. Yet…

Wouldn't it be nice to finally let my hair grow? It had been short since I was an infant. And did I really need to wear a damn jacket and tie every day? The guys who went to the Bronx High School of Science didn't wear them. They had long hair and torn jeans for crying out loud!

Focus got up to leave. "I'm telling you, Dave. You don't—"

"Know what I'm missing. I know. You fucking tell me that all the time—you, Chino, everyone."

"Yo, chill, David. We're just talking."

"Is that what we're doing?"

"You too wound up, man. I'm going home."

"Yeah, keep working on those business skills."

When my next report card came, I ranked Number Thirteen.

***

And that, dear reader, is how the rest of the school year went down—and downhill. Each subsequent marking period saw a lower ranking, a lowered expectation. I assured myself I wasn't doing that bad. Indeed, I ended freshman year in the top five percentile of the school; my grade point average a 90.5, my lowest ranking 23. From the outside looking in, one would think I'd lost my freaking mind thinking I had any problem at all. But something inside had clicked off for me.

When I first envisioned spending more time in the block, I figured I'd continue to work hard in school. I just wouldn't work *really* hard. At the very least, I wouldn't worry about it. Who needed the heartburn? As any athlete will tell you, the problem

is not being at the top, it's *staying there*. It's retaining the edge
to overcome the forces, real and imagined, that want to take
you down. It's working *even harder*. And that, I told myself, was
something I didn't need in my life.

However, I had gone beyond merely not worrying about
school. I was now on the cusp of no longer caring about it—and
that was entirely new territory. This realization didn't come as
an epiphany moment or anything like that, more a slow dissolve
to black.

In retrospect, it all seems ludicrous, that I should be so con-
flicted over such petty shit like wanting to go to hooky gigs and
growing my hair. That's one of the things about being a teenager, though: the ease with which you can slide into despair. A
pimple equals death, a jacket and tie a chokehold.

I can see now that I was also being impacted by the times,
an era of rebellion where change happened rapidly, identity
challenged and made over repeatedly. The summer of 1970
was set to begin, the first summer of the new decade. The social and political rebellion of the 60s carried over and gained
force. Struggles for civil rights and against the Vietnam War
had become embedded in American culture. Everyone was on
the move: women, lesbians, and gays, Third World communities, as we were called back then.

One time, a guy from the block named Raphael asked me
to consider joining the Young Lords Party, the foremost revolu-

tionary Puerto Rican group of the period.

"The Young Lords talk about socialism and all kinds of deep stuff," Raphael said. "But they back it up too." He went on to explain how the Young Lords fought for Lincoln Hospital, and how they even swept the streets when people got pissed about how little the garbage trucks came around.

I could only nod in agreement, not knowing enough to disagree. I felt stupid, actually, being so out of touch as to be unfamiliar with the Young Lords, or groups like them. Raphael wore a Puerto Rican flag on his shirt and thanked the Young Lords for reminding him to be "proud to be Boricua."

I nodded again. All I could say was *baya*—right on.

"Yo, David, aren't you, like, this really smart dude in school?"

"Who told you that?"

"Nobody. I just hear things. People be like, 'That David is a brainiac.' It's alright, bro. I ain't gonna make fun of you."

"I'm not that smart, Raphael."

"If you ain't with the people's struggle then you must not be."

When it came to that type of smart—politically smart—Raphael was right. Overall, I didn't ask questions or seek answers, and my closest friends were the same way. We'd remark how "shit in the world was getting crazy" and then go off to play handball or eat pizza. While keenly feeling the assassinations of Martin Luther King Jr. and Robert Kennedy, I was never involved in political activism of any kind: never attended a demonstration, never went to a rally, never held a picket sign. In my fifteen-year-old eyes, there was the world, and there was my life, which was crazy enough.

There was also my neighborhood: the South Bronx, which had been a solid, working-class community, poor in sections with a high concentration of people on welfare, but filled with strong families and aspirations of a better tomorrow. The '60s brought on deeper racial pride and cultural awareness, and hope clung to the air. But the era also brought on an influx of heroin, crime, and poverty. In the '70s, the South Bronx would ignite, literally and figuratively.

Drugs played a central role in the drama unfolding on the block. Yet they came with a strong appeal, a magnet promising never-ending nights of girls, partying and fun. That's where my buddies were heading—and me with them.

CHAPTER SIX

You ever feel like life's going by in a blur, you're both there and not there? That's what the summer of 1970 was like for me. There and not there.

I began smoking cigarettes more often, alternating between Kools, Viceroys, and Newports. I mostly bought "loose," the name given to single cigarettes sold in bodegas. The smoking addicted me to Bazooka gum, which I smeared on my hands to hide the smell from my parents, making my fingers pink and sticky as taffy. Not once did I worry about the scent on my clothes because I didn't smell it. Nor did my parents, probably because Pops' two packs a day of Parliaments gave our apartment a permanent aroma of tobacco. As for drinking, I graduated from beer to nip-and-tucks of blackberry brandy, Bacardi rum, and an occasional pint of MD 20/20—a cheap wine affectionately called Mad Dog. My favorite wine became Boone's Farm, which was light and fruity. (Remember Boone's Farm? What about Malt Duck?)

That summer I finally smoked marijuana. I had wanted to try chiba, which was allegedly laced with embalming fluid. Chiba got you "fucked up," a goal far nobler than merely getting high. But Chino and Julio insisted I try out mota, a pot so strong that a nickel bag netted you only three skinny joints. Plus it got you *"real* fucked up." Big difference.

***

For my grand christening, the three of us go to Chichamba, a humorless playground adjacent to the 7 Up factory on 132nd Street near Cypress Avenue. We sit on a park bench facing the approach ramp to the Triborough Bridge, cars and trucks hurtling by New York style: cursing and honking. Chino quickly gets to business rolling a joint.

"Hey, David, let me ask you something since you're the brainiac," he says. "What does chichamba mean?"

I crack up. "You know, Chino, in all the years we've known each other, you've never asked me the meaning of something."

"It wasn't important."

"Well, I think chichamba comes from the word *chichar*—to fuck."

"That's perfect," Julio says. "'Cause we're gonna get seriously fucked up!"

"You mean real fucked up!" I add.

We laugh and watch Chino roll. The guy has it down to an art. First, he lays out two sheets of *Bambú* together so that the each sticky end of the sheet shows. After tapping the mota into the paper, Chino removes all the seeds and twigs with the precision of a diamond cutter. He then rolls the joint so tight that nary a crease is visible.

"I got a BIC lighter!" I say.

"Go Dave!" Chino says, passing me the pencil-thin joint.

"Since you're the virgin, you get to fire it up."

I light up and inhale deeply. Chino instructs me to hold my breath to keep the smoke in. "Okay," I croak, feeling like I'm underwater. After a few seconds, I whoosh the smoke out. My friends cheer. I drag on the mota again.

"Stop hogging the shit up," Julio says, taking the joint from me and repeating the sacred inhalation ritual. Then he passes the j to Chino. And on it goes.

It doesn't take long for the marijuana to kick in. I feel hallucinatory, giddy. I gaze across the ramp at the Millbrook Houses, framing the skyline like a hazy silhouette. Squinting, I find my building, 165 St. Ann's Avenue.

"I see my apartment window!" I yell as if I've discovered the Seventh Wonder of the World.

"You got fucking x-ray vision now!" Julio says.

When I peel myself off the park bench, my body wobbles, a human Slinky.

"I feel... I feel..."

"What do you feel, Superman Dave?" Julio asks.

"I feel..."

"Tell us, man!" Chino says.

I break into the James Brown song, "I Got You (I Feel Good)."

> *Whoa! I feel good, I knew that I would now*
> *I feel good, I knew that I would now*
> *So good, so good, I got you.*

Julio mimes the horns and Chino does the James Brown slide as I sing at the top of my lungs. Passing cars honk in solidarity.

I fall back on the bench and shake my head. "Why didn't you guys ever tell me what I was missing?" This provokes more howls of laughter, after which we all close our eyes and let the word spin. We begin telling snaps. "I went to your house and stepped on a match, and your mother said, 'Who turned out the light?'" And "I went to your house and asked your mother what's for dinner. She said, 'Steak and peas.' When she gave me the plate, I said, 'Where's the steak?' She said, 'Under the pea.'" We laugh for hours.

Energy spent, I get the "munchies," my first experience with that classic marijuana side effect. Chino and Julio are famished too, so we trudge to the Cuchifritos Restaurant on 138th Street near Brook Avenue, where I order my perennial favorite: a plate of pig tongue, pig ear, pig stomach, pig intestine and, in a nod to health, a boiled green banana. There's something just so Puerto Rican about eating cuchifritos, and ordering the food in Spanish makes it extra special: "*Una orden de lengua, guajo, oreja, morcillay y un guineito, con gravy.*"

***

The rest of the summer of 1970 was more of the same. I was getting stoned virtually every week and having a total blast, and that's just the God's honest truth about it. Mota didn't just make me laugh and give me the munchies. It heightened everything: every sensation, every emotion. Even my intellect felt deeper, particularly when watching television shows like *The Outer Limits* or seeing movies like *Planet of the Apes*, which was showing to packed houses at Loew's National on 149th Street and Bergen Avenue. Who needed school?

It took some major-league pouting, but I eventually convinced my mother that I shouldn't be in honors class in my sophomore year. Mami knew about my steady drop in school rankings, of course, but I told her that the work was simply getting harder and harder and that I was still her *hijo inteligente* and that sometimes you just had to ease up on the pedal before you went a little cuckoo.

Giving up on honors bothered her, though. She wondered: If you're not with the best how can you be the best?

Good question.

"You have to trust me," I said.

"I want to, *mijo*. But it's easy to be stupid, too."

Good answer.

CHAPTER SEVEN

Alas, Mami was right. Before long I was whining and sulking again, chafing at my jacket and tie, hating my hair, which had grown thick during the summer but had to be cut before school started. I had given serious consideration to the possibility that a relatively lighter workload at Cardinal Hayes would make it easier to toughen out my remaining three years there. In fact, I told myself, my decision not to be in honors could be the smartest thing I'd ever done. But the opposite happened. A lighter academic load didn't make matters easier at all. I mean, the work *was* somewhat easier, but it didn't take much for me to end up not wanting to work at all.

At first, the sophomore-year classes at Hayes were kind of fun, thanks to a new buddy named Armando, the classic underachiever. Armando received grades that were both uproarious and, I'm sure, embarrassing. One day, Brother James read our grades aloud as he handed back our English composition exams. "Wilson, 86; Driscoll, 74; Perez, 85; Rosado (dramatic pause), 7." A chorus of "ooohhhhs" filled the classroom, including from Armando, who looked at me and said, "It's just a fucking test."

Most of Armando's friends attended Taft High School, located close to Hayes and across the street from his apartment building. According to Armando, they nagged him constantly to "stop wearing monkey suits to school and rejoin the human race." I related to that. I also related to Armando because I myself was now on the long and winding road to underachievement. Tradition and what remained of pride in good grades prevented me from sinking too far down in the subjects I enjoyed, like English and trigonometry. My first report card ranked me in the triple digits, as did the following one. Then I went into free fall, and I did nothing to stop it. It's as if I had been split in two, like in an out-of-body experience. Part of me was planted in the day-to-day, living out my increasing misery. Another part of me was hovering above, watching in bewilderment as the "real" David stubbornly refused to shake off the blues. My brother George noticed the change in me.

"Looks like you're giving up, little bro."

"I'm just tired, that's all."

He snickered. "How the mighty have fallen."

"I got nothing to be ashamed about, Papo. Sometimes you just need a change."

"Not if it's downhill."

My declining work ethic affected my running track too. I had become the top sprinter on the Hayes team, and because I could also win or place in middle distance races like the 880-yard run, Coach Slater had one day put up a notice in the locker room that read: "David Perez is the most versatile runner in New York City."

For a brief moment, I regained my ditty-bop and walked the halls of Hayes with pride. But the moment lapsed quickly. Soon I began skipping practices, tired of all the drills, the work it took to remain so "versatile." I lost my competitive fire.

Part of becoming an elite runner was that the competition also became elite. I was racing against some intense Road Runner dudes, prominent among them this cat named Mora from Bishop Dubois. He had the best kick I'd ever seen. By the time Mora hit the finish line, he had gained so much momentum that if the tape weren't there, he would have kept sprinting clear to California. I could never beat Mora, or anyone like him, and after a while, I just stopped trying. Whenever I looked for my own extra kick, I found the tank empty.

The tank totally emptied with my grades. In my final report card of the semester, I ranked 366 out of 680 students.

***

Mami was livid that I'd given up on Hayes; that my grades plummeted so rapidly and spectacularly. She was also hurt. Both my parents never completed their education, having to shoulder too much family responsibility while growing up in their respective rural homes in Caguas, Puerto Rico. Mami cooked and did laundry for a family of eight, as well as for the men who helped till the land. She left high school in her junior year. Pops was taken out of school in the middle of the third grade and has worked his entire life ever since. His first paying job came when he was 12 years old, working on a migrant farm in Pennsylvania with his older brother, Ricardo. He worked from dawn to dusk picking spinach and earned $2.50 a week.

I assured Mami, again, that I knew what I was doing.

"Stop saying that! You're not fooling anyone!"

I hated seeing my mother angry. She was barely five feet tall, but she was a giant in my eyes and grew noticeably taller when she yelled. I hugged her and promised, promised, promised that I wouldn't let her down, that I still wanted to attend a "good school." Which was true. I hadn't stopped caring about a good education. It simply wasn't going to be in another Catholic school, with its over-the-top rules and regulations. That part of my life was decidedly and blessedly over.

After several days of tossing around various possibilities, I chose Aviation Vocational School, which was still all boys back then. My friend, Melvin, a fellow St. Luke's alumnus, went there and said it was a good school. Melvin was one of the more solid guys in the block. His aspiration was to one day work as an airplane mechanic at JFK or LaGuardia airport. He also boxed for St. Mary's Recreational Center as a flyweight, tipping the scales at 106 heavily ribbed pounds.

Mami was skeptical about Aviation but looked at the bright side. "Maybe you'll become a pilot!"

Well, not quite. Aviation required shop classes every semester, and since I'd spent a year and a half at Hayes, I had to make up for it by taking three two-hour shop classes *all at once.* If I had any inclination toward being a mechanic, harbored any desires to learn aerodynamics and the working of carburetors, engines, and airplane wings—or, as my mother hoped, become a pilot for Eastern Airlines so I could fly her to Puerto Rico— they were dispelled immediately and utterly. The sheer volume of shop classes made me brain dead, rendering it impossible to overcome my "not being mechanically inclined," as one teacher kindly put it. After not being able to weld a straight line, my teachers and, grudgingly, my mom were clear that I wasn't fixing anything or flying anywhere.

Academically, I did well enough in the two non-shop classes I took to appreciate that, while Aviation had a good reputation, it was light years from a school like Cardinal Hayes. More than once during English composition, I thought: This stuff is way, way too easy.

Unfortunately, just like what had transpired at Hayes, the lighter load resulted in my being smack back into the territory of not wanting to work at all.

***

On May 28, 1971, I turned 16. Weeks later the school year ended, and I got my first summer job at a daycare center on 149th Street and Jackson Avenue, two blocks from my parents' first tenement flat in the South Bronx, where oversized cock-roaches reigned supreme and the boiler barely broke a sweat. I worked in a classroom run by an obese woman named Annie, with jowls that appeared to have melted on her face.

Annie was reasonably nice to the children, but her patience wore thin easily. This one kid named Marcos had the regrettable habit of punching himself in the face whenever he got upset.

One time, Marcos was crying himself into a face-pummeling frenzy. Annie stared at him. "Let me know when you're finished."

Marcos didn't relent, leaving me to finally intervene and end his misery. I hugged him. "Come on, Marcos, that's enough. It's okay." Marcos sniffed and wiped snot on his sleeve. I hugged him again. Annie scowled and waddled away.

Upon cashing my first $60 paycheck, the first item on my agenda was a new look, starting with a shag haircut, the latest rage of the times. Julio, naturally, already had one, as did several guys from the hood. Forget *Saturday Night Fever*. Puerto Ricans had shags way before John Travolta hit the scene. In fact, 'Ricans were ahead of the curve on a lot of fashionable trends of the time, from clothing to haircuts. As I mentioned before, it was the Nuyorcians who pioneered slam poetry and the spoken word movement. As for music and dancing, we were kicking it from salsa to boogaloo, from ballrooms to discos, from jazz to the seeds of what would become hip-hop.[1]

---

1 Juan Flores' book, "From Bomba to Hip-Hop: Puerto Rican Culture and Latino Identity" (Columbia University Press 2000), gives a terrific and comprehensive history of the unique contributions of the Puerto Rican community.

The hair salon I picked might as well have been a discotheque: blaring music, colored lights, a mirrored ball on the ceiling. When my turn arrived, a woman with a grip like a nutcracker gave me a shampoo, lathering and massaging my skull.

"First time?" she asked.

I nodded.

"I like virgins."

Hmm.

After that, my assigned stylist, a stunning blonde in leopard tights, led me to a high barber's chair and—with scissors, comb, and turbo-charged blow dryer—sculpted my newly grown hair into a work of art. When she handed me the mirror, the renovation was complete: I had a shag! Layered like rows of brown feathers.

After helping me shop economically at Delancey Street, Focus went with me to buy shoes at a boutique shop on 59th Street and Second Avenue. "This is where rock stars go," Focus said.

I believed him. The guy working in the store looked like Mick Jagger with bigger lips.

"Can I help you darling?" he said to me.

"Uh, I need shoes."

He stared at my Converse sneakers.

"Something taller perhaps?"

"Sure. Size eight please."

I tried on various shoes and made my pick. Julio was pleased with my choice.

"You did good today, bro," he said.

At home, I tried on my new outfit: pink flowered shirt with big lapels, beaded necklace, a gold glitter belt, pleated gray mohairs with a long silver keychain dangling from the pocket, and two-inch turquoise platform shoes.

Mami was aghast.

"¡Ay dios mio, parece un payaso!"

Pops, sitting in his recliner chair, looked up at me and then down at my shoes. "It's all stupid."

***

Thus began two years of one party after another: Sweet
Sixteens, house parties, and school dances at both public and
private high schools. At first, it was a balancing act to not twist
my ankles in platform shoes. But soon I was jumping and spinning and gyrating in my new self-proclaimed Disco Dave per-
sona. At this point I was hanging with different friends from
the neighborhood and school. Actually, not everyone was technically a friend. In fact most weren't. This period of my life was
a swirl of action and people. If it were a film, it would be shot
as a montage of quick-cutting scenes: David at a hooky gig in a
Prospect Avenue basement apartment stoned and slow dancing
with a girl who's half-asleep. Cut to David in shop class, who's
totally asleep under an airplane engine.

While I was admittedly having a great time exploring drugs,
girls, and parties, I also discovered that getting high did have its
scary side, and the experiences were enough to make me want
to cool my jets.

***

Experience number one: I'm hanging with my friends Edgar and Harold, trying out a new strain of marijuana, Acapulco
or Colombian or something or other from somewhere south of
the border. We score the pot at a seedy tenement building near
132nd Street and Brown Place. The dealer is on the top floor,
and he hands us the nickel bag through a sliding window on the
door, much like in a confessional booth or prison cell.

After smoking a couple of joints, the three of us agree that the pot is whack and could probably use some embalming fluid. We go outside. Standing there is a plainclothes Latino cop, gun drawn.

"Freeze!" he yells.

Edgar runs, and the cop grabs him. Edgar, all 100 pounds of him, fights the cop off with his fists and dashes down 132nd Street. The cop exhales and, gun at his side, turns to Harold and me. I'm shaking but trying to appear brave.

"You all were trying to steal the fucking pigeons!" the cop yells.

Harold and I stare at each other in disbelief.

"What pigeons?" I ask.

"On the roof. I *know* that's what you all were trying to do."

"No, man," Harold says. "We were just smoking herb."

The cop glares at us. "You sure you all weren't trying the steal the fucking pigeons? The owner's been complaining about kids trying to steal his fucking pigeons."

"You mean like in *The Birds?*" I say.

"Fuck the birds!"

"I'm telling you, we were just smoking herb," Harold repeats.

"Yeah," I add. "None of us have seen or heard any birds, I mean pigeons."

The cop sighs and holsters his gun. I exhale.

"Get the hell out of here," he says.

A couple of blocks away, I turn to Harold. "Why did you

keep saying that? *Only* smoking herb?"

He shrugs. "Because it was true."

"Yeah, but what if he wanted to bust us for that?"

"He only cared about the 'fucking pigeons.' You were the one with the stupid joke about the bird movie, so shut up."

I shake my head. "That was something with Edgar. Jesus, you'd think he was on the lam or something."

"He fought and ran 'cause he had a dime bag of heroin in his pocket."

"Jesus H Christ, we all could have gotten busted for that too!"

"David, come on, we're okay, okay?"

But I'm wasn't okay. All I can think about then was being in a cell with a heavily tattooed con and telling him I got rolled because of stupid pigeons. He'd lick his lips and say, Oh really?

***

Scary experience number two: my first acid trip with two guys I'll call Shadow and Moby. The three of us are getting ready to go to a new disco called the Volcano. I'm wearing my other fabulous disco wardrobe: tight black tank top, red latex belt, blue jeans with the crease stitched on, and mustard Marshmallow shoes.

The year is 1971 or '72. I forget which. The disco scene is a full-blown explosion. Cavernous clubs have sprung up all over the city with names like the Sanctuary, the Forbidden Fruit and the Inferno, reflecting the melting pot that is New York City:

Italians from Brooklyn, 'Ricans from the Bronx, Blacks from Harlem, Asians from Chinatown, vets home from Vietnam, wall-to-wall bodies dancing to a pounding sound system that reverberated in the bathrooms. The DJs didn't use a mixer, just two turntables going from jam to jam: *Soul Makossa* by Manu Dibango, *It's Just Begun* by the Jimmy Castor Bunch, and *I Can Understand It* by New Birth.

Shadow takes out three tabs of blue dot, a type of LSD.

"Three tabs?" I ask.

"It doesn't have a lot of speed. It's cool, David. We'll get to the Volcano and bug out."

"But a whole tab?"

"It's weak."

I down the tab with a swig of beer, and Shadow and Moby follow suit. After only a few minutes, we all realize that Shadow's dealer had bullshitted him. Blue Dot had, in fact, a lot of speed, certainly enough that we shouldn't have swallowed a whole tab.

At first, there's a sense of disorientation laced with pleasure, colors and sounds heightened to the nth degree. My heart rate increases and the living room seems to literally pulse, walls like lungs. Then the sensations become too much.

"Whoa!" I say.

"Let's get out of here," Shadow says.

We get on the subway feeling paranoid. Shadow complains

that he's falling off his platform shoes. Moby keeps muttering, "I don't know, I don't know." My shirt is uncomfortably damp and the train clanks so loudly that it feels like it's inside my skull. We arrive at the club at 11 p.m. Hardly anyone is there.

"A dormant Volcano," I say.

"Fuck it, let's dance anyway," Moby says.

"I'm taking off my shoes," Shadow adds.

The disc jockey puts on *Jingo* by Santana. The little crowd that's there is on the dance floor, and three of us join them.

Discos were one of the few places where guys could just boogie down without necessarily having a partner. And that's what we did. After a few hours or so, the acid winds down to a manageable roar. I have a splitting headache and tell the guys I need to go home.

"Let's do this again!" Moby says.

CHAPTER EIGHT

Back at school, junior year at Aviation, my grade average nosedived to 74, and I flunked 11th-year math, my first failing grade ever. I was surprised I'd gotten a 62, considering I rarely showed up for class. At first, I pumped my fist in triumph. Failing was hip, defiant—or so I had long thought—and now I had done it. But you know what? It wasn't all that. No trumpets accompanied my "accomplishment," and I never shared that report card with anyone either, just like I hid ranking number three at Cardinal Hayes.

In fact, the more I thought about it, the more I mourned this state of affairs. My striving for knowledge had devolved to the point that I was watching TV game shows like *The Match Game* and *Hollywood Squares* to exercise my intellect. I stopped reading books altogether and rarely watched the news—and even then, primarily for sports coverage. If it weren't for stimulating shows like *The Twilight Zone* and *The Outer Limits* my mind wouldn't have gotten any brain food at all.

Ah, but life can be a grand paradox. Just as I vowed to chill out with getting high and do better in school, along came two arenas that would salvage and define me for decades to come: radical politics and writing. The latter arrived in the form of my first short story—one that sprang from me, as opposed to a school assignment. I don't recall any inspiring moment that led me to the writing. It just happened. Appropriately enough, since I was hanging out more with what I considered the tough crowd, my story was about gangs. I titled it, "As the City Sleeps."

My brother George drew the "cover" with colored magic markers. On the upper left of the lined composition paper was a couple in bed kissing (no, not me) with the tagline, "They love because they want to..." A diagonal line then cuts across the page, and on the bottom right side is a snarling Puerto Rican guy with an Afro and a machine gun (no, not me) with the tag line "...And kill because they have to!"

"As the City Sleeps" totaled 25 handwritten pages. I still remember the opening lines: "The blanket of night hovered over the urban jungle. It provided the perfect security blanket for prostitutes, junkies, and thieves. It was a typical night in New York City."

The story borrowed shamelessly from the film *The Dirty Dozen*. Indeed, that was the name of our 12-member gang, all of whom were modeled from real-life friends. But I only used their nicknames. I called myself "Brain," an artistic license since it was cooler than Brainiac. Other characters included Chino, Dill Pickle, Smokey, and Soaky.

Here's the synopsis: One of our gang members is ambushed and almost killed. We find out it was the Mafia. We hesitate to take them on until someone in our gang says, "What are we, punks?" Of course, we're not. So we find and kill one of their guys by cutting off his balls. The Mafia retaliates and kills one of our guys in equally gruesome fashion. After making love to his *mujer*, our leader Tito declares war and we attack the Mafia's headquarters, which is posing as an electrical factory in Queens. But the mob guys are too organized and too well armed. Only two of our Dirty Dozen gang makes it out alive (no, not me).

Depressed over what happened, Colorao, the only survivor without a bullet wound or bandage, is walking in the neighborhood when a guy comes over and tells him that a mutual friend got beat up by a gang. "Time for revenge," the guy says. Colorao shakes his head no. The friend gets angry. "But we're not punks" he insists. Colorao shakes his head again and walks away.

Then comes the last line of the story: "And the night echoed, we're not punks, we're not punks."

I passed the story around to a few of the guys, who loved it and wondered if a career in Hollywood had suddenly become possible—for them. Tito got a little pissed that he got killed and swore he was "too fast, too cool" to have been machine-gunned. Chino complained that he should have had the love scene instead of Smokey. All of them said I was a good writer.

I see now that "As the City Sleeps" was an attempt to keep some of my intelligence and imagination burning. At the same time, I was bringing my friends to life, proud of them even as I showed the potential tragedy of wrong priorities. There were important stories in the Millbrook Houses and the Mott Haven community, a noble side to the street guys, and I wanted to honor them in a way, perhaps even save them. Many of them I couldn't. As it turned out, though, the writing was an unconscious way of saving myself.

***

While I was personally uninvolved and often uninterested in radical politics as a whole, the turmoil of the '60s-'70s era invariably found its way to my consciousness, even it was simply becoming aware. Besides Raphael Ramos talking to me about the Young Lords Party, there were brothers from Millbrook touting the Black Panthers and Malcolm X, shouting "Fuck the Man" at every opportunity, and squaring off against the cops on 137th Street. The signs of the times were everywhere, and socialism was a word everybody heard.

That said, radical politics in earnest came to me courtesy of Milton Vera, whom I met at one of St. Luke's "Youth Sundays," a type of rap session initiated by the trendy Father Ryan to talk about whatever was on your mind. At first, I went there to shoot the bull and play checkers while stoned on mota, which made me take the game so seriously that my challenger would always get angry and yell, "Just make a fucking move already!"

After a few Youth Sundays, with nobody left who wanted to play checkers with me, I got to know Milton, who grew up near St. Mary's Park. Milton was several years older than me and had once helped manage a club with Joe Namath, the famed New

York Jets quarterback. At the age of 25, he'd already hatched five kids, three of which were girl triplets. Milton considered himself a proud Marxist. His explanations of how capitalism worked were especially inventive.

"Look at that shirt you're wearing, David."

"My shirt?"

"Yeah, your shirt. What's it made of?"

"I don't know, a little silk. You want to touch it?"

"No, I want you to think about it, *compañero*. Who made the silk? Who stitched the shirt together? How did it get into the store? Who sold it to you?"

"People?"

"Right. People. Working people. Our people. We make everything, David, and yet the boss man owns everything."

"Yeah, well, but I own the shirt."

"But that's the *only* thing you own. The capitalists own the silk and the factories that spin it, and even the ships that bring them here. And why is that?"

"Because they have more money?"

"Right. And their money is called *capital*."

"Ah, hence the word capitalism."

"Very good. Under socialism, it all works the same way, except there are no bosses to own everything. Isn't that a better deal, *compañero*?"

"Maybe."

Talking with Milton was kinda fun and challenging. I could never come up with good arguments against socialism, except that to say, Hey, we live under capitalism, and it isn't *that* bad. I mean we're here, right? We eat okay and party a lot, and I still have a cool shirt, and that's nothing to sneeze at, right?

I soon realized, however, that I really didn't know squat about socialism. The only book I'd ever read—or been forced to read—on the topic was *What You Should Know About Communism and Why*, put out by Scholastic, the magazine publisher, and aimed at junior-high school readers. Brother Raymond had assigned it to our eighth-grade class. The front cover featured a menacing photo of the Chinese Red Army, marching in goose-step, hell-bent on taking over the world.

Milton said that was all "bourgeois propaganda." Marxism and communism were "world systems," studied and practiced by hundreds of millions of people. The Soviet Union had the largest landmass in the world, China, the largest population. And besides, Milton added, "the world could use some taking over."

What talking with Milton did make me feel bad about, though, was never doing anything "to change the world." And it wasn't that I had to look far. The world was burning right in my own backyard. Arson had grabbed the South Bronx by the throat, most of it carried out by landlords in a deliberate scorched-earth policy. Soon the South Bronx would become home to the busiest fire stations in the United States, and the population would decline by 50,000 people in the span of a few years, a stat usually attributable to war.

Milton said he went to all types of demonstrations and protests, and that it was important to get involved. To his credit, he never pressured me to do the same, once emphasizing that I needed to get my own life together first.

"You get high a lot, right David?"

"A bit. What, you don't get high?"

"Never. That shit eats your mind. A couple of the guys here at Youth Sunday got the heroin monkey on their backs. Too many of our people are OD'ing."

"I'm laying off the dope," I said.

"Shit eats your mind."

"Watching the acid, too."

"Another shit that'll eat your mind!"

"Calm down, Milton. You're, like, screaming."

"I just hate it when people waste their lives, David."

"Well, I'm not wasting mine, okay?"

"We'll see."

***

I'm not going to lie and say that I "saw the light," shook off the drugs, and rode off into the sunset. But I did manage to keep the getting stoned part manageable, and I started to take school seriously again. Mostly. When senior year rolled around,

I became attentive and showed up to every class. Mostly. I even scored a couple of 80 grades. I wasn't soaring, but I wasn't sinking either.

I even did a brief stint with the Political Club at Aviation, where I plagiarized Milton's ideas as my own. I enjoyed the debate aspects of the club, the arguing for the sake of arguing. One day, I used one of Milton's explanations about capitalism to show the system's "contradictions." I was going at it with this dude named Ace.

"The capitalists have to pay workers the least money possible in order to make the most profit possible, right?"

"Possibly," replied Ace. "Although—"

"Wait, let me finish before I forget. Okay, so that's the capitalist. He's over here on this side. He's on my right."

"Why the right?"

"Because he's the boss!"

"Oh I get it," Ace said. "Left, right—very clever."

I plowed on. "But the bosses also have to charge the most possible for their products in order to make the most profit. Pay less, charge more, irreconcilable contradiction."

"So they have a sale."

"What?"

"A sale. The bosses put their products on sale, and then the workers can buy them. Problem solved."

I stared at Ace, dumbfounded. The guy had a good point.

My mom bought everything on sale. So did Pops. And what about Focus and his business skills at Delancey Street?

Ace crossed his arms. "Capitalism works. Any more arguments, Mister Marxist Man?"

"Let's talk about your shirt..."

***

Eventually, Milton's talk about the importance of workers and "the power of the proletariat" got me to think about my father, specifically his job in a meatpacking factory. For Pops, work was everything. If you subtracted sleep and most weekends, work is where he spent most of his life. It was the reason he got up at five every weekday morning. And never once had I asked, "What's it like there, Pops?"

Well, that wasn't a hundred percent true. I did know something about what happened to the meat when it was processed at the factory: the chemicals and additives, the transformation of beef into "100 percent USDA shit," as Pops so eloquently put it. None of that, however, prevented Pops from bringing home said meat from work. It was cheap, and that's what counted. Of course, we always ate it.

I hardly talked to my friends about what my father did. His official job title was "meat pumper." As a kid, I mentioned that to a couple of friends, and they goofed on it big time. Pumper? What does he do, fuck the meat?

CHAPTER NINE

I arrive at Stars Meatpackers factory on a Saturday morning, a day my father's working overtime. Cattle carcasses hang on hooks attached to overhead conveyor belts, while workers in white lab jackets and firemen's rubber boots yell and sing as they push the skinned animals through the peeling green metal doors. Stars Meatpackers is located on Ganesvoort Street in lower Manhattan, across the West Side Highway from a Department of Sanitation dumpsite.

A side door opens, and my father's head peeks out.

"Come on down!" he says, sounding like Bob Barker from *The Price Is Right.* The rare times Pops calls in sick and stays home, he's glued to the TV set watching one game show after the other, calling them all just one gambling casino. "You bet and win money. Same thing."

"Hey old man," I say, greeting Pops at the door. He's dressed in his usual work outfit consisting of a plaid flannel shirt, blue chinos, and brown-leather shoes. A few months ago he began wearing glasses, a decision he had put off for years. We shake hands.

"So you came," he says.

"I told you I'd be here."

"I know. But things happen."

The door is near the workers' locker room, and we enter.

"Lots of sawdust here," I say staring at the floor.

"Puddles too."

"I've noticed. So, you wanna show me around?"

We go into the locker area, and my father hands me a white lab jacket smeared with dried blood. I laugh and put it on.

"I feel like a doctor," I say.

"Same thing," says Pops, pointing to bloodstains. "But doctors don't have to wear these."

He passes me a pair of rubber boots that weigh a solid five pounds. I thank him and slip the boots over my sneakers. Pops puts on his boots, and we trudge out of the locker room and into a small room with a stainless steel table. On top of it is a basketball-sized side of beef.

"Ah, this is where you pump," I say.

"No, I work inside the floor. But here I'll show what I do."

Pops explains that both the bosses and the union can't allow unauthorized people to be inside the main factory; if an accident happened, there would be hell to pay. And accidents did happen, all the time. Broken limbs, sprained backs, people knocking themselves out on the wet floor, fingers sliced...you get the picture.

"I'm fine here, Pops."

Even in the small room, the noise is deafening. But after dancing in discos with speakers the size of Redwoods, I'm used to it. It's different, though, the sounds of pulleys and hydraulic pumps. Water hoses set on stun.

With hands covered in tiny scars, Pops demonstrates his technique. He holds the lump of beef and pulls out a vein with a special type of scissors. Wrapping the vein around his fingers, he uses his other hand to inject the vein with a fearsome needle filled with water. Then he does it again with a couple of other veins. Wash, rinse, repeat.

"How many times you do this a day?" I ask.

"I don't count. Maybe a hundred. Maybe seventy-five."

"That's a lot of veins.

"You get used to it."

"I imagine you would."

"It's my job, *hijo*. It's what I do."

Mami told me once that Pops had once been offered the foreman job. He refused, claiming it was too much work, too many headaches. But my mother and I knew the truth. Becoming foreman meant my father would have to write and file reports. He couldn't do that. Pops was functionally illiterate.

"And now I can say I've seen you do what you do," I say, patting Pops on the back. "Can you take a break? Maybe we can get some coffee or something."

"I go ask the foreman, and then I come back."

I wait at the table and think of all the hard work my Pops does. And not just him but everyone in the factory, cogs in a churning and noisy assembly line that begins at the loading platform and ends in meats that are cut, sliced, processed, and loaded onto trucks that deliver the final product to stores and restaurants, so we can finally load it into our bellies. I don't yet know what I want to be in my life, but it's definitely not this. Noble visions of "the salt of the earth" aside, this is some freaking hard work, dirty and smelly and dangerous.

How many workers wish they weren't here? Does Pops?

At a nearby coffee shop, we munch on grilled-cheese sandwiches and drink café con leche. Pops usually eats lunch in the locker room on the food Mami makes him, but he left it in the refrigerator for another day.

I stare at Pops as he wolfs down his meal. Like my mother, he's 38 years old. His black hair has thinned.

"It was really nice coming here," I say. "Felt like seeing another world. Your world."

"Won't want to live here."

We talk a bit about the different jobs the workers do, how everyone is dependent on everyone else. One breakdown in the production line and everyone suffers.

"It's good you got a union," I say. Pops agrees. Without the union they'd be just like the meat, sliced and diced and shoved out the door.

We polish off the rest of our food and drink in silence. Outside, delivery trucks honk and barrel down the streets. The Meatpacking District, as the area is called, bubbles with factory work by day and prostitution by night. The area earns its name.

I stare at my father, who's lost in thought. After sliding down a hard road of drinking and gambling, he'd only recently gotten his act together. He began mending his ways after one day driving home in his 1958 Impala and not remembering how he'd done it.

"I could have killed myself and never knew it," he'd told my mother the following morning. Mami threatened to move out if he kept at the bottle. *"Tu y su hijo son dos sinvergüenzas,"* she said.

When Mami told me how she'd put my father and me in the same sentence, calling us two fools, I knew it was time to start getting my act together too.

"You know Pops, part of me coming here was to see you in your element, in the place you've been going to since I was born."

"How old are you now?"

"Seventeen."

"Time goes fast."

"That's what I mean. You're my dad and all that, and I know about your job and how you've been working since you were twelve years old—"

"Eight years old."

"Okay, eight."

"It's really four years old."

"Fine. Let's make it from the womb. Right. I know that. But what about other things?"

"Like what?"

"I don't know. Like, okay, here's something I was just thinking about: Do you like your job?"

"It's a job."

"Yeah, but do you *like* it? Do you like working in a meat factory?"

"Work isn't for fun."

"It could be, though."

Pops shrugs. "I hardly ask you, David. How's school?"

"I'm doing okay."

"You like it?"

"Good one, Pops. Sometimes, yes. Sometimes no."

Pops pays the check, and we get up to leave. As we put on our spring jackets, Pops looks at me and says, "Remember: As long as you go the right way, you never go the wrong way."

I laugh. "You always say that."

"Always true."

CHAPTER TEN

The Sunday after visiting my dad, I was feeling great and decided to go for a nice, long walk. Let my feet guide me wherever. The weather was overcast and brisk. Good spring walking weather.

First I went to the Big Park. It was early morning, so not many people were around, just a few kids playing in the big swings. There used to be eight swings in the park; only three remained. The slides and seesaws were still intact, but the sandbox was now empty of sand; had been for a while. I crossed Bruckner Boulevard and went through Chichamba, which was growing more desolate-looking by the hour, a playground on downers. On the bench in front of the chain-link fence, empty cellophane bags of heroin were scattered among assorted Hostess Cupcake wrappers and used condoms. Someone had also placed a thin foam mattress in the park.

I crossed 132nd Street and got on the mile-long footbridge leading to Randall's Island, a 480-acre island park in the East River that connects to East Harlem, the South Bronx and Astoria, Queens. It was in Randall's where I discovered I ran fast, back in the seventh grade during track practice. I'd always enjoyed walking the footbridge, which ran alongside the Triborough Bridge. As you approached Randall's, the view grew increasingly scenic and green, with its plentiful sports fields and vast lawns. I'd kissed many a girl under the island's starry skies.

But Randall's Island had also succumbed to the increasing hardships of the time. On the off-ramp from the Bronx footbridge, just underneath where it ended, was a square opening that used to be covered with a metal lid. No longer. *Tecatos* from the block had pried the lid loose and converted the catacomb-like place inside into a heroin shooting gallery, adorning the dirt floors with candles. I should know because I'd been there. Not to shoot up, but because I was invited by friends who wanted me to see their "new clubhouse."

"This is like one of them chambers in one of them pyramids, right?" Skinny Vinnie said when I first visited.

"Only dustier," I said.

Vinnie took out his spoon and syringe. "Maybe I'll be buried here, man. Become one of them mummies and shit."

"Maybe you will," I said.

But no one was at the clubhouse that Sunday morning, although it wouldn't have surprised me if Vinnie or one of his minions had decided to crash in the place or had simply passed out. Or died.

I continued walking through Randall's and arrived at the area where we had track practice. I found our former "starting line," a long crack on a cement path lined with trees. The finish line was wherever Brother Lawrence placed a garbage can, a distance of approximately 60 yards. The hundred-yard marker was

the Discus Thrower statue, close to Downing Stadium, home
to sporting meets and an occasional rock concert.

I gazed out at the statue. *Why not?* I thought and began
jogging toward it, feeling a little weird as my Converse sneakers
made a plop, plop noise on the concrete. It had been forever
since I had ran in anything other than track shoes, except for
the few times I played softball and the one time Julio and I ran
from the housing cops after getting snagged smoking herb in
the Big Park. I'm not sure if the cop actually chased us. All we
heard was, "Stop! Police!" and we hauled ass.

I reached the Discus Thrower statue, now marked with
graffiti, one of its arms amputated. I was only slightly winded.
Good to go. I stifled an urge to just sit in the grass and smoke a
Newport, and instead jogged back to the starting line. This time
I sprinted, not full throttle but working the legs and pump-
ing the arms. The lungs burned when I reached the statue. I
coughed. *Still got it, right David?*

I jogged back to the starting line. One more. I threw off my
nylon jacket and ran. Hard. Fast. Coach Slater screaming, "You're
beautiful!" as I reached inside for the hallowed kick, still stored
there, waiting. I poured it on at the end and whooshed past the
dismembered statue, a fellow symbol of times past. I stopped in
front of a bench and bent forward, hands on knees, heart beating so hard I can hear it. It sounded beautiful.

As I went and retrieved my jacket, my goal became clear,

sharp as crystal. I had planned to do well in school and simply get a regular high-school diploma. Reach the finish line and be done with it. No, that would be a waste, I told myself. I'm going to go for the gold. Get myself a New York Regent Diploma, the highest academic diploma attainable. That would mean taking two special tests: one in math, one in English. "Piece of cake," I said aloud. "All I need is the kick."

I lit up a Newport and headed home.

***

In what had to be a world record in cramming, I studied my ass off for the tests. Mami was thrilled to see her son at home night after night, buried in textbooks and exam guides.

"Aye, mijo, por fin," she said.

Pops was starting to be home at nights more, too. He was also happy to see me studying, going the right way.

The Regent exams were hard, but I shouldered through, determined not to repeat the experience four years ago at Bronx High School of Science, when I took the Specialized High School Admission Test and gave up even trying to find the answers. This time, I smirked at the demonic word problems sneakily thrown in alongside the algebra, trigonometry, and geometry questions. But I ended up guessing anyway. Ditto with graphs.

With the English exam, a strange thing happened. I discovered I was bored with it, particularly the essay. I only wanted to write what interested me. I don't recall what the suggested topic was, only that it seemed terribly irrelevant. But I plowed through, determined to pass. Confident. Strong.

CHAPTER ELEVEN

On May 28, 1973, I turned eighteen. I was officially a man, old enough to vote and fight a war, but not old enough to drink. Back then, the drinking age in New York was 21, but I had long learned how bullshit that law was. At neighborhood bodegas, I'd seen kids as young as eight buying beer and rolling paper.

A month after manhood, I graduated from Aviation Vocational High School with a standard diploma. I almost passed the Regents but missed each test by a few points. Still, my final overall school average had zoomed to an 80. My aim had been to get to the finish line with a kick, and that I did. I didn't get the gold, but I tried.

I still didn't have a clue what I "wanted to be." At one time I had considered going to the Albuquerque University in New Mexico with Harold, my close friend from Aviation and fellow adventurer with the pigeon-obsessed cop. The school was Harold's choice because it had a great reputation and was located "in the hot desert with hot babes." He wanted to become a doctor; I would decide my future when I got there. In a strange way, it made sense: South Bronx, Southwest. But I chickened out and wanted to remain close to home, unaware that New Mexico would enter my life big time decades later.

Which left the question open: Now what?

After celebrating graduation smoking a couple of joints with a few buddies at Chichamba, I caught up with Milton Vera at a local bar on 143rd Street and Jackson Avenue.

"Congratulations to the graduate!" Milton said when I entered the bar. The other patrons cheered and raised their drinks as a toast.

"My treat," Milton said. "Whatever you want."

"Are they going to card me?" I asked.

"Are you kidding me? One, I know the owner. Two, I'm buying the bar."

"No shit? When?"

"Soon. We gotta talk some figures."

I ordered a rum and Coke. Milton yelled, "Make it two" and told the bartender to make the drink strong for his "favorite Marxist buddy!"

The bartender laughed. "As long as you pay with capitalist money."

A TV set atop the bar was showing a Yankees game. I had the munchies, so I gulped down the bowl of peanuts in front of me.

Our drinks arrived, and Milton raised a toast.

"To David!"

"To David!" I echoed.

The rum and Coke was strong but great. I took a second sip and ate more peanuts. Milton looked lost in thought.

"What you thinking?" I asked.

"How I never finished high school. Did you know that? I was lucky because I was business smart. Always have been. There's a lot of kinds of smart, David, and you don't have to pick one or the other, street smart, business smart, school smart. Shit, you can be all three."

"Now there's a thought," I said. "We should add political smart too."

"To the proletariat!"

We finished our drinks and Milton ordered another round. My head was spinning, but in a nice way.

"So tell me, David, what you are going to do now?"

"Ah, that is the question. I'm thinking maybe Hunter College. Take a course in Puerto Rican Studies, maybe something in philosophy or economics so I can debate your communist butt."

"Anytime, *hermano*. But you think more like me than you think."

"You think?"

"I do."

I finished my drink. My buzz reminded me that I was still kind of aimless. All I really had were possibilities.

Outside, the night air was warm and damp, the beginning of another New York summer. Fire trucks sounded off in the distance, and people were hanging on the stoops, playing dominos, laughing, staring ahead. Lost. Or not.

CHAPTER TWELVE

Okay, this is the part of my story where I need to omit names and condense events because it involves relationships and privacy that I want to honor. Suffice it to say that in a two-year span after graduating from Aviation, I ended up getting married, having a daughter, getting separated, and joining the U.S. Navy. With Milton's help, I also landed my first full-time job in the duplicating department at SSC&B, a large advertising firm in midtown Manhattan, where I learned to operate an A.B. Dick 360 Offset Press and troubleshoot Xerox machines—nice skills but not anything I felt destined to do, whatever that was. I became an expert on fanning paper.

I enrolled in Hunter College like I'd planned, but could only take evening classes. Between work and hanging out with guys from the block, time only allowed for a few courses.

I started with Sociology because, well, it felt like something smart people studied to get smarter. For the life of me, I don't recall learning anything of value. My other course was Anthropology. What possessed me to take Anthropology remains another mystery. I suppose it was another topic that made me feel smarter simply for taking it. What I did retain, though, is an appreciation for other cultures and older civilizations, a subject that would fascinate me more in the future.

The birth of my daughter Belinda on March 20, 1974 brought temporary joy. I did all the daddy things, like changing her diapers and feeding her Similac and tickling her and making cute animal noises. I called her Munchkin and marveled at her soft *pipón*, that precious mound of baby belly tailored for snuggling. But if I wasn't ready for marriage, I was even less ready, at the age of nineteen, to be a father.

So, I joined the Navy. I guess I looked at it as a way of being responsible, of manning up and providing for my child, of seeking a new adventure. And, yes, it meant getting away from... everything.

I was urged to enlist by Red, an ex-sailor and former head of the Savage Seven, a short-lived street gang that I'd tried out for once by standing inside a circle waiting to be attacked by their seven fist-clenched gang members. Before the initiation, I'd asked if this meant they'd change their name to the Savage Eight. Their prison-tattooed leader, Big Blue (Red was in the Navy then), cracked up, said "Go!" and punched me in the face. Down I went as the rest of the group pummeled my curled-up body. Afterward, they all congratulated me for "taking it like a man." I thanked them and told them I had other plans.

Red laughed when he heard the story. We were drinking rum and Coke in the living room of my new walk-up apartment on 138th Street and Cypress Avenue, right next to St. Luke's Church. Across the street was an empty lot where three buildings used to stand, before the rising arson claimed them.

"I'm glad I got out of that shit," Red said. "Joining the Navy was the best decision I ever made. I pulled my shit together, had a nice paycheck, traveled overseas and got me some nice medical and education benefits. Going back to college and shit one day."

"You say shit a lot, Red," I said.

"Maybe you should just check it out, man."

"Sail the Seven Seas, huh?"

"At least it's going somewhere."

Point taken. I finished my drink and sank into my Salvation Army sofa. "Maybe you're onto something, Red. Maybe I should check the Navy out. But what if I don't like it?"

Red lit up a joint and said there were always "loopholes and shit" around it.

"Like what?"

"I'm not sure, but you'll find out."

I ran the idea by Milton. He thought I had lost it.

"Jesus, David, you're thinking of enlisting in the goddamn imperialist Navy?"

"Oh boy, here we go."

"Haven't you heard anything I said?"

"I did, Milton. Every word. But I live *here*, right? Land of sour milk and no honey, as you like to say. I agree with that. I agree I gotta read more and get involved and stuff. But I have a daughter, this job pays shit, and like that dude Red said, if I find

I have to get out then I'll get out. I'm taking care of business."

"Don't become no cog in the war machine, David."

"Vietnam's just about over, Milton."

"I don't know, man. I think you've lost your freaking mind."

Red advised me to visit the same guy who recruited him, Chief Petty Officer Jose Sanchez, a fellow Puerto Rican assigned to a recruitment office in Flushing, Queens. Sanchez greeted me with a chest full of medals and a dangerously creased uniform. When he asked about my grades in school, I told him the truth: that I used to be at the top of my class but had slacked off. He suggested I sign up for the Nuclear Program, which entailed passing a special test to see if I have the chops for the program.

"This isn't about bombs is it?"

"It's about nuclear power and nuclear submarines and the highest technology around!" replied Sanchez, practically saluting. "Those who enroll in the program start at a higher pay rate, an E3. Regular recruits start at E1. Let's do the math."

We did. I'd earn an extra $45 a month, a lot of money in those days, plenty for child support payments and for me to open my first savings account.

"Not too shabby," I said.

"You also do basic training in San Diego. Sunshine and beaches, as compared to the Great Lakes, where everyone else goes to freeze their asses off."

The guy knew how to make a pitch. Then he told me the fine print.

"The only hitch is that you have to sign up for six years."

"Six? I thought it was four."

"It usually is, but like I said, this program is special. La crème de la crème. Guys like you. So it's six years."

Major bummer. Could I last that long? How much of that time would be spent cooped up in a submarine? I thought about Captain Nemo in the flick *20,000 Leagues Under the Sea*. Didn't life in a sub drive him crazy? The pay was a major incentive, though. And California!

The following week I took the Naval exam for the Nuclear Program and passed. "One of our highest scores ever!" crowed Sanchez, who had put a small Puerto Rican flag on his desk.

"Now what?" I said.

"I'll put it the paperwork and hook you up."

"Sound good."

"Welcome aboard, *Boricua!*"

Mami was mixed about my joining the Navy. She had warned me about getting married so early, about not being ready to be a father. But she always tried to give me the benefit of the doubt, being that I always seem to avoid falling 100 percent into the precipice. I was always her *"hijo inteligente"* who couldn't stop doing *"cosas estupidas."*

"You just have to stop being unhappy," she said.

Pops repeated his mantra: "If you go the right way, you never go the wrong way."

He gave me $100 and I said thanks. We cracked a beer together and drank.

My farewells to friends were uneventful. Julio had basically disappeared after moving from the neighborhood. No one seemed to know where he'd gone. Chino married a woman from the Dominican Republic and lived upstate with her and her three children. As for the rest of the guys I knew and hung out with, it was a phone call here, a toke of a joint there, and a few *saluds!* to an unnamed future.

When I went to say goodbye to Belinda, she was asleep, curled up in her crib with her rattles and stuffed animals. A mobile hung overhead, casting shadows in the dim light of her small room. I kissed my Munchkin goodbye. On her first birthday, I would be in boot camp.

CHAPTER THIRTEEN

March 1975. I arrived at the San Diego Naval Recruit Training Command in the late evening and barely slept on a cot covered with a coarse gray blanket and a pillow the size of a walnut, bewildered alongside 80 other guys from all over the United States. At five a.m. a couple of burly men burst in, flipped on the bright fluorescent lights and started banging on steel garbage cans with metal pipes.

"Get the fuck up! Come on, move it!"

I fumbled around and flung on my dungarees and shirt. As I struggled with my shoelaces, one of the screamers stormed over to my bed and yelled, "I said, move!"

In my rush, I left my blue leather jacket on the bed, and ended up standing outside shivering in the cool dark air. Screamer Number One came out of the barracks holding my jacket. "Who the fuck left this?"

I raised my hand and he tossed it at me. "Where you from, boy?"

"The South Bronx!"

"Oh, excuse me, the South Bronx!"

Screamer Number Two laughed. "We have a tough guy in the crowd," he said, parking his bullfrog face inches from mine. Then he added: "You're a long way from home, son. Welcome to the United States Navy."

After a few more rounds of yelling the sun came up, and I
officially began week one of basic training, called "P-Week"—P
as in processing; P as in *pendejo*. I endured a battery of medical
and dental exams, and innumerable inoculations. Then it was
on to the legendary haircut. Staring at my reflection after being buzz-sawed, all I could think was: Is this what I really look
like? Everything on my face looked bigger, as if magnified by
a fun-house mirror. My slightly crooked nose covered half my
face. My full lips were cymbals. One brown eye was noticeably
rounder than the other eye. When did that happen?

Every day was busy, starting at 0400 and ending in total
exhaustion at 2000—that's four a.m. to eight p.m. in "fucking
civilian time." I was issued clothes, hygiene items, shoe polish,
sewing kit, t-shirts, shorts, suntan lotion, a green guard belt,
and an ID card. I learned to fold a bed sheet so tight you could
bounce coins off it. I learned how to make my pants into a
floatation device while treading water. I learned how to stencil
my name on clothes. And I marched. Everywhere. Right face.
About face. To the rear.

The last day of P-Week featured a lecture on the Uniformed
Code of Military Justice by a fire-and-brimstone officer straight
out of central casting: granite-carved face, Popeye forearms,
straight spine, shoes shining like a crystal chandelier. He pointed to the huge American flag on the classroom wall, took a deep
breath, paused, then spoke.

"See that flag? That's the flag that represents our country."

He was talking slowly, emphasizing each word; crisp, sharp, just like his uniform. The guy knew how to work a room. He pointed to the blue and the stars.

"See that? That represents the blue sky that flies over our beloved country."

Next came the white stripes.

"See that? That's white for the purity that symbolizes our country."

He inhaled deeply, icy-gray eyes boring right through us. His teeth were clenched like he wanted to beat up somebody. He pointed to the red stripes, voice rising.

"See that? That represents the blood that we shed defending our country."

Cue the thunder.

"And who's going to defend our country?" he roared.

"*We are!*" we roared back, including me. For an instant, I was itching for a howitzer to blow up America's enemies. Let me at 'em, goddamn it!

The moment passed. I was shaken, confused. What the hell just happened to me? The lecture on the UCMJ continued, and I took notes. But my mind was back in New York, back at the job, listening to Milton Vera talking about the "imperialist military." Warning me about propaganda and how effective it was. "Don't let them eat your mind, David," he had said.

Did I just get my first dose of gung-ho propaganda? If so, the officer was effective and precise. He played me and I let myself be played.

***

As luck would have it, I was mistakenly given the job of yeoman, a kind of secretary who performs general clerical and record-keeping duties during basic training. Our company commander, Captain Marshall, a five-foot five former Navy Seal built like a fire hydrant, had asked who the fuck was this Perez who used to be a clerk? No one spoke up, so I finally raised my hand, thinking maybe my recruiter had somehow put that information in my file.

"Why the fuck didn't you answer me?" Marshall bellowed.

"Sir, I—"

"Never mind. You got clerical experience?"

What the hell. "Sir, yes, sir!"

He handed me the "purse," a 10-by-12 rectangular container with a lid to hold papers and forms.

"You're now the yeoman, Perez!"

"Sir, yes, sir!"

I later discovered that a Filipino named Perez was the guy who used to work as a filing clerk. When I asked him why he hadn't spoken up, he said, "I didn't want job. Too much work; too little English." (My unit included 20 Filipinos, shipped to the U.S. straight from the Philippines. They spoke broken English and were a tight-knit group.)

Being yeoman turned into a blessing. I received perks, such as not having to perform grueling galley duty during "service week." I had a small desk in the captain's private quarters, where I filled out assorted forms, maintained daily logs and entered scores on our weekly written tests. Still, boot camp was plenty tough. There were endless inspections and drills; it was hard *not* to get something wrong. I did a round of push-ups for having a button undone. One guy had to run around the barracks with a mop over his head for leaving a stain in the bathroom. Another had ever so slightly folded his socks wrong, so was forced to push the balled-up socks with his nose while crawling on the floor on his belly, his hands clasped behind his back. You get the picture.

Overall, I felt lucky, though. Despite the brutal aspects of basic training, Captain Marshall was actually a bit laid back. He joked and often let a mishap go. For every guy he told, "Get down and give me 20," he told another guy, "Don't worry about it, it's just a blanket." Since I worked in his office, I sometimes saw Marshall with a faraway look in his eyes, like maybe he didn't want to be there either. He reminded me of Brother Steven, my GI Joe clone sixth-grade teacher at St. Luke's Elementary School, who had a passion for paddling kids and hanging them by their jackets on a coat hook. But when he taught biology, Brother Steven would become misty-eyed, especially when explaining "the holy reproductive process." He ended up leaving St. Luke's and the Brotherhood completely.

Five weeks into the nine-week basic training, Captain Marshall ended up leaving too. Not only had he virtually stopped doing inspections, he'd also come in a few times sniffling his nose and looking stoned. He would yell, "Let's march!" then change his mind and say, "Forget it, I'm going home."

Base command eventually got wind of Marshall's "highly irregular" behavior and replaced him with the snarling and muscled Captain Thompson, who introduced himself by hurling one of our guys against a wall for "looking unhappy" with the change in command.

"My job is turn you all into men!" Thompson screamed.

But in a surprising twist, at least to me, Captain Thompson's determination to transform us into men made us equally resolute to prove that we were indeed already men, thank you very much. Within a week, we marched with such precision that our company received a banner for Best Marching Company. We felt proud, and, yes, I felt proud too. No matter how hard I'd fought it before, there was something intoxicating about the synchronized sound of boot leather on concrete, the whoosh of 65 pairs of arms and legs filling the air like the wings of a giant bird.

As basic training drew to a close, we received two evenings of "liberty." Naturally, we mostly got drunk at local bars. The last night on the town, I was on a bus back to the base, shit-faced with a few of my mates, celebrating our pending return home. Captain Thompson was with us, having decided to "join my fellow Navy men." We started making fun of some of our marching songs, laughing hysterically over the punch line, "You're fucking A we like it here!" Thompson laughed right along, springing up and down in his seat like a jack in the box. For the briefest of moments, all the divisions and privileges of rank dissolved. We were just a bunch of guys getting smashed on a Saturday night.

The last day of basic training was filled with emotion. Boot camp was intense and I choked up saying good-bye. It startled me, this verge of tears. With the exception of kissing my daughter Belinda goodbye, not once in any of my farewells to my South Bronx friends did I cry, or even get close to crying. Did this mean, gulp, that I was now Navy material? That boot camp accomplished its vaunted task of making me proud to be in the service? That I'd grown to fucking A like it here?

On the plane ride back to New York City, I was in my all-too-familiar adrift zone, wondering where the hell I was going.

CHAPTER FOURTEEN

When I saw Belinda, her smile said, "Daddy!" but her eyes said, "Daddy?" We went to Coney Island, and I brought her a plastic dolphin. Belinda did remember me, of course, but it felt a bit strange as if she sensed my visit was temporary, that I'd miss her second birthday too, and the one after that. Or maybe it was just my imagination.

During my two-week leave, I stayed with my parents. My bedroom remained barely touched, except all the posters of Willie Colón and Led Zeppelin had been replaced with gilded-framed baby photos. The closet was stuffed with extra pillows and bedspreads. Since when did we have so many?

Mami exclaimed that I looked *"muy guapo"* in my uniform and thanked the heavens that I'd finally put on a few pounds, thanks to heaps of starches, gravy-soaked Salisbury steak, and heavily boiled vegetables. I now tipped the scales at 135 pounds, with bigger biceps and toned pectorals. Pops said I "looked like a man."

George had landed a job as an illustrator for Marvel Comics. For years, he had practiced his craft without ever taking an art class. Like me, George had married young and regretted it, having to endure a miserable job as a bank teller to make ends meet. But he kept at his dream.

"I'm finally doing what I was meant to do, Dave!"

"That's great, Papo," I say, meaning every word.

"Drawing *The Fantastic Four!*"

"Amazing."

"Now it's your turn to be amazing, little brother."

"I'm working on it."

"I hope so. You seem to be taking the scenic route."

Being in San Diego was the first time I'd been away from home for so long. Our family went to Puerto Rico at least once a year, but that was for two weeks at most. This time, I'd been gone for over two months. Everything in the neighborhood seemed magnified, and it wasn't pretty. The projects were more run down, the streets dirtier, the empty lots more numerous. A sense of gloom had settled in like soot. So-and-so got mugged. So-and-so was in jail. Did you hear about Cheetah? Got shot after ripping off this dealer in broad daylight.

Everybody was going on with their own lives. Oh, a handful of us got high and drank and did all the welcome backs. But a rift had formed. I was in the Navy. I was "gone." I was going on with my own life. But to do what, exactly?

My return to San Diego approached rapidly. I panicked. Everything was happening way too quickly. This was home, even with all the mess. I had unfinished business here. What it was I didn't know. That's why it was unfinished. What on earth was I doing in the freaking military? It's not as if I could just quit, the way I did in Cardinal Hayes. Where was the loophole

Red talked about?

One guy in Company 071 had gotten kicked out early on in basic training when he appeared mentally incompetent, walking around like a zombie and barely speaking. After inspecting his footlocker for the second time and still not finding anything folded, Captain Marshall gave up. "Get him out of here," he said to another officer who was helping with the inspection.

Our whole company watched as our catatonic bunkmate was led inside a car to be discharged. He turned around and ever so briefly flashed us a smile. We all looked at each other in astonishment and knew. He had faked the whole thing.

Is this something I would have to do? I wondered.

For advice, I turned to the ever-reliable Milton. He was, it seemed to me, everything I was not: settled, responsible, purposeful, committed to a set of ideals that, deep inside, I knew meant something. But was he something I wanted to be?

"What should I do, Milton?"

"It's hard, David. You just gotta figure it out. Didn't you say that? That you'll figure it out?"

"Yeah."

"If you come back I'll find you a job here again. Something always comes up." Milton was still the mailroom supervisor at SSC&B, the advertising firm where I'd worked. Every time I used to stop by, the guys in the mailroom were either arguing or laughing, usually at the same time. It looked like a very cool place to work.

I told Milton about the officer and the American flag and how for a moment I wanted to blow some commie's head off. He smiled.

"It might have been mine!"

"No way, Milton, you're a friend."

"That's the thing, Dave. We're friends, and I'm on your side. This is important. We're workers, *compañero*. We make the world go round."

"Like my shirt."

"Like everything."

The day of my departure, I toyed with the idea of going AWOL; hide somewhere until I figured out what I wanted to do in life. The idea must have worked subliminally because I missed my flight back to California and had to scramble to find a plane that flew me to the Naval Base in Norfolk, Virginia, where I connected with a twin-engine jet that took me to San Diego. Looking out the smudged window, I felt familiarly at sea again. It pissed me off no end.

CHAPTER FIFTEEN

In the summer of 1975, I officially began the nuclear program at the Naval Training Center, with a chip on my shoulder. I was designated Fireman for no discernable reason, and my first class was electrical theory. I hated everything about it: the droning teacher, the ohms, the watts. The class reminded me of the brain-numbing shop courses I languished through at Aviation, where the only thing I enjoyed was looking like a mechanic; wearing coveralls with a greasy rag hanging out of my pocket.

Somehow, I obtained my certificate of completion. Please don't ask me how. I was back to the drugs again, big time, mainly Colombian gold and Moroccan hashish, provided by two new buddies: Williams and Kolchak. Williams was a jumpy Black brother from New Orleans with a bushy beard and no moustache. Kolchak hailed from Poland and lived in Chicago. He was the prototype slacker—bony body in perpetual droop. The three of us were housed in the same dorm building and shared a common "How did I get here?" about life in the Navy.

The weeks and months dragged on. I took another course or two. Maybe. I don't know. The military police busted me twice in the space of a week. The first time, the MPs found a smoldering hash pipe on the ground next to me. I swore it wasn't mine.

"It just happened to be there when you guys came along.

What are the odds, huh?"

They stared at me like I was an alien from another planet.

"Well, maybe we better confiscate this contraband," one of them said, putting the hot pipe in a plastic bag.

"Is that a real evidence bag?" I asked.

"Just watch where you're walking, okay?"

"Sir, yes, sir!"

The second bust occurred with the pipe in my mouth, and I was placed in Alcoholics Anonymous, of all things. I introduced myself as a "drug abuser," which elicited nods of sympathy and more than one confused expression. Over the weeks at AA, I was genuinely moved by their tales of hardship and woe, of lives spiraling out of control, of men drinking until they blacked out. But I felt immune to it, almost above it in a strange way. They had a drinking *problem*. I had no problem at all, except being in the Navy when I didn't want to. In my final session, I told them how I had went for a walk in the park and realized, "Who needs drugs when you have *real* grass to enjoy, right?" I related the indescribable joy of "getting high on life" and they saluted my epiphany, stating how proud they were all of me. In retrospect, I think they knew I was full of crap. Real addicts can smell bull-shit a mile away.

More time went by and I got busted yet again. This time, the base police snagged me in my room on base, where I had inexplicably left the window open so that all of the San Diego

Naval Training Center could smell the wafting marijuana.

"What is it with you, sailor?" one of them yelled as I sulked in a nearby cell.

"I'm a fireman."

"You're an idiot."

Later, a stern captain ordered that I be sent to a drug rehabilitation center in Miramar, a base not too far from the San Diego facility. Williams and Kolchak told me I'd scored big time.

"Yo, Dave, I hear that if you don't get rehabilitated there you'll be offered a medical discharge with full GI benefits!" Williams said. "That's too sweet."

"I'm jealous," Kolchak said.

It dawned on me. *This is the loophole I've been searching for, my ticket out of the Navy!*

"But this means I have to *not* be cured," I said.

"You want to stop getting stoned?" Kolchak asked.

"No."

"Well, there you go," said Williams.

So off I went to the Naval Drug Rehab Center in Miramar, California, established in 1971 as a "response to acute concern with the epidemic of drug abuse that developed in Southeast Asia," according to the handout I was given. Most of the guys in Miramar were heroin and cocaine addicts. When I arrived, one of them asked me what I was in for.

"Pot and hash."

"That's it?"

"I also do acid."

"That's it?"

"Yeah, but I'm addicted to all of it."

"Fucking Navy."

I was classified a "polydrug abuser" and hit it off immediately with my fellow inmates. Many had been stationed overseas in South Korea, the Philippines, and other countries. A couple of guys were from Brooklyn. Most were adamant about kicking the heroin and cocaine monkey off their backs. Compared to them, my monkey was a baby chimp. But privately I was thrilled to be rubbing elbows with serious *tecatos*. In my naïveté, these rogue characters represented the ultimate fuck-you to authority. I especially envied and admired their boldness. A neighborhood addict named Tutú was stealing goods off the backs of trucks *while they were waiting for a red light to change.*

I actually had tried heroin once with Focus. We both knew its risks so decided to play it safe by snorting it, rather than mainlining or skin-popping. Focus ended up throwing up. I ended up with no high at all, wondering if perhaps my twice-broken nose—courtesy of playing tackle football without a helmet and running face-first into Fat Ray's thundering knee-caps—had rendered the dope impotent. Whatever the case, both Focus and I vowed never to do heroin again.

That said, I reveled in my resume-building time with Miramar's hard-core addicts. I knew their lingo, and we shared many a war story.

At my first session with my counselor, Miss Collins, she scratched her head.

"What are you doing here, David?"

"What do you mean?"

"The way you are in group. You just seem too smart for all this. That somehow you don't really belong here."

I agreed with her and added that I didn't belong in the armed services either. She nodded and repeated her surprise at my being here. "Must have been a clerical error."

I was insulted. I did drugs!

Miss Collins scribbled on her notepad and chewed on her pencil. "Where do you think you do belong, David?"

"Not here."

"But where?"

Ah, that was the crux of the matter, wasn't it? Where exactly did I belong? The clock ticked loudly on the wall. Miss Collins sat in her chair and waited me out. She wasn't not much older than I was, mid to late twenties perhaps. Her light brown hair was flipped at the ends.

"I guess I have to find out," I said.

***

The weeks passed. There wasn't much to do beyond the general cleanup duties in Miramar, so I had plenty of time to ponder the question. None of us were confined to base. If I wanted to take a bus into nearby San Diego, I could. But I chose to stay put.

One evening I was lying on the grass outside the main housing unit, doing some much-needed contemplation. What, as my counselor so astutely asked, was I doing here? I didn't consciously plan on getting busted and ending up in Miramar. Yet, it appeared to be my ticket home. I was sober for the first time in months, which was sort of nice. My final review was only a few days away, but I still planned on not being rehabilitated.

I inhaled deeply. Unlike New York, the southern California air was clear, adding brilliance to the night sky overhead. I saw the Milky Way, and felt that I was noticing it for the first time, not counting school trips to the planetarium in New York. It had been a while since I prayed and I found myself talking to the heavens. *What should I do, God? How about some sign?*

I inhaled again, and suddenly felt exhausted. Exhausted over being constantly "lost." Lost in high school, lost becoming a young husband and father, lost in the Navy, lost during leave back in the Bronx, and now lost again. *I'm only 20 years old, and I've lived a lifetime. Check that. I haven't really lived at all.*

***

I saw Miss Collins again.

"So your final evaluation is coming up," she said.

"Yeah, tomorrow."

"How do you feel about it?"

"Fine. You?"

"Come on, David. Let's get serious. Have you thought about our last conversation?"

She stared at me and we did the traditional therapy dance: She led with a question, then waited as long as it took for me to follow with an answer. Pretty effective.

"I think about it all the time," I finally said. "It's more like I know where I don't belong than where I do, more a getting away from than a going to. Does that make sense?"

"Perfect sense. That's often the most important thing, David. Realizing where you don't want to be can help illuminate the road ahead."

I laughed. Therapists and counselors had a language all their own. The group leader at Alcoholics Anonymous spoke the same way, of "light" and "dark" and how a negative pole can highlight a positive pole. I tapped my feet.

"Want to tell me anything else?" Miss Collins asked.

I proceeded to tell her everything. My history of top grades and my subsequent free fall, my years of partying and getting stoned, my becoming a husband and father, the push and pull of my neighborhood. Hearing myself speak, I was struck by how whiny and pathetic it sounded, like I was beating myself up. I was reminded of that summer job at the daycare facility, of four-year-old Marcos punching himself in the face whenever he got upset.

"What are you thinking about?" Miss Collins asked.

"Nothing. Just this stupid kid I once knew."

She nodded.

"Well, our time's up, David. Do you know what you're going to say in your evaluation?"

"More or less. Can I ask what you're going to recommend?"

"Just what I've shared with you, David. You don't belong here that's for sure."

I nodded. "Thanks."

She smiled. "I don't like secrets."

At my final evaluation, the reviewing officer asked if I had any statements to make, as if waiting to pronounce sentence. I coughed and began my rehearsed script: that I would continue to be a polydrug user because I just couldn't tolerate being in the armed services, that it wasn't the Navy's fault, God forbid, but my own unfortunate and lamentable weakness. I choked on my words at appropriate moments and looked him square in the eye. The captain cleared his throat and looked over my record.

"Miss Collins seems to agree with you."

I remained at attention as he sipped a glass of water. Outside the window, an aircraft carrier was visible on the pier.

"I'm giving you a general discharge under honorable conditions," he finally said.

"Sir, I thought I would get a medical discharge, sir," I said.

"You're not sick."

"But—"

"Get out before I put your sorry ass on a submarine."

I saluted and left. I was angry but quickly realized that a general discharge meant I could still keep my GI benefits. I could continue college and let the Navy pay for it. It was something.

***

Two days before being let out into civilian life, I was cleaning a room that used to house the library. Reaching up to dust the top shelf of an empty bookcase, my hand bumped into a book, hidden near the back wall. I took it down. It was *Introduction to Socialism* by Leo Huberman and Paul Sweezy. Well, well, what have we here?

The book was free of dust so it couldn't have been in the shelf for long. Plus the library had been empty for a while. So, who put it there? None of the guys in rehab ever hinted of radical politics. We generally agreed that "the Navy sucks" and that "officers suck." But those were hardly controversial views.

I began imagining that somehow God had heard me. That the book was the sign I had asked for. That my future laid somewhere in the world of Marxist politics. I mean, I'm given my last assignment at Miramar and I just happen to find a book called *Introduction to Socialism?*

I stuffed the book in my back pocket, and then got scared.

What if I'm caught? What if it's a trap? A shuffling sound came from outside and I froze. But no one knocked or tried to enter. Exhaling, I placed the book back in the top shelf and left.

On Dec. 16, 1975, I packed my duffel bag for the last time and waited for the bus to take me to the San Diego airport. I never discovered the identity of the closet socialist, if indeed there was one. No matter. I felt wonderful. I still wasn't 100 percent certain where I belonged. But as Miss Collins had said, sometimes it's knowing where you don't belong that counts.

CHAPTER SIXTEEN

Nine months after enlisting in the Navy, I was back in New York City, ready to begin anew. I saw my daughter Belinda every other weekend, taking her to the Bronx Zoo, Central Park, and countless movies. I also brought her to a few house parties to show her off to prospective new girlfriends, who cooed when they saw a divorced father taking care of his cute daughter.

True to his word, Milton hired me as a mailroom clerk at SSC&B, which was on its way to becoming the seventh largest ad agency in the world. The company had recently moved to a new building near the United Nations, occupying nine floors with a workforce in the hundreds. The mailroom now employed ten guys, a few from our South Bronx stamping grounds. These guys came and went a lot—some because they grew tired of the low wages, others because they would "forget" to return to work after a two-marijuana-joint lunch. It didn't take long for me to land a job there.

The work itself entailed sorting through an average of five duffle bags of mail a day, stuffed with letters, magazines, catalogs and assorted parcels. This was 1976, pre-email and pre-fax. We then placed the sorted mail in metal-wired carts filled with labeled hanging folders, and twice a day delivered mail throughout the nine floors. We also processed outgoing mail, filling up a mailbag of our own for the post office to pick up in the late afternoon. Other duties included wrapping and shipping items for air transport. Fed Ex was just beginning as a company, so we used a variety of overnight couriers. Doing messenger trips throughout Manhattan was the part of the job I enjoyed least. Each time I delivered a package to another firm in midtown Manhattan, I had to enter through the freight elevator, the white-collar version of the back of the bus.

Still, for the most part, I was happy and content. Rarely did a day go by without some great jokes and a nice sense of camaraderie, with Milton supervising our ship smoothly and fairly. When I said to myself, "I know what I'm doing," I truly meant it, perhaps for the first time in my 21-year-old life.

When my paychecks accumulated enough, I was able to rent a small studio apartment in Hell's Kitchen, the first in a string of apartments throughout New York City, each lasting an average of three months. I moved for different reasons: it was too far from the subway; it was too cold; the rent was too high and had to be paid on time. I moved so often my friends nicknamed me Gypsy. Fortunately, my possessions were meager: a couch that folded into a bed, a chest of drawers, a small TV, a small stereo system, and minimal cookware.

In the midst of work, Milton and I resumed our political discussions. He agreed that my "finding" *Introduction to Socialism* was likely divine providence.

"Marx works in strange ways," he said.

"You mean God."

"Him too. Here, I got something for you."

Milton reached into his briefcase and pulled out *The Communist Manifesto*, by Karl Marx and Frederick Engels.

"Oh, you just happened to have this," I said

"I told you. We work in strange ways."

At about sixty pages, *The Manifesto* seemed more a pamphlet than a book. "This is like the communist bible, right?" I said.

"Except that it's true."

"And a lot shorter."

The Manifesto proved to be a tough read, even at sixty pages. It had quite a gothic feel to it: images of "a specter haunting Europe." Capitalists like "sorcerers who have lost control of their powers." It was almost poetic. Fiery too. The capitalist class "pitilessly tore asunder" feudal relations of the past, replaced all human relations with "callous cash payment," and created a world market "in its mirror image." This description of capitalism would be verified in real life time and time again, I would discover, including by those who still supported the system.

Nevertheless, there was plenty I didn't understand, particularly the section about the Fabians and other European entities. Marx and Engel might as well have been speaking Greek.

I asked Milton about it. "You really understood all that stuff they wrote?"

"Not all of it, but I got the sense of it. You have to study it, read it slowly, make notes."

"You know what the book reminded me of? All the stuff I read as a kid about other worlds, and ghosts and things mysterious. That's what economics is to me sometimes. Like a secret vault."

"This is about here on Earth."

"Well, here on Earth is fucked up."

"My point exactly."

***

Meanwhile, I enrolled in Hunter College and took courses at night, using my educational benefits from the Navy to pay for the classes. Since I'd only lasted nine months, the money only covered two courses.

My first class at Hunter was Puerto Rican history, which I chose to get more in touch with my culture and heritage. Despite annual trips to the island, and my legions of Puerto Rican friends, I didn't know much about the history of the homeland. I knew of Operation Bootstrap, the 1947 program initiated by the Unites States that transformed the island's economy from an agricultural base to an industrialized one. And of course, the food and the music. But its social and political history?

My teacher, Ms. Torres, turned out to be an advocate for

Puerto Rico's independence from the United States, and her favorite tactic in proving the island was a U.S. colony was to cite
newspaper clippings from the mainstream press that described
Puerto Rico in those very words.

"But it's called a commonwealth," I had objected early on in
class.

"We have nothing in common with U.S. wealthy owners,"
Ms. Torres replied.

"Everyone I know there has a car."

"*Coño*, David, was does that show? That we can drive?"

Ms. Torres reached into a folder and pulled out an editorial
from *The Wall Street Journal* titled, "America's valued relation-
ship with its oldest colony, Puerto Rico."

"Case closed," she said.

The things I never knew about the homeland! The 1868
rebellion against Spanish colonialism, called *El Grito de Lares*,
where the Republic of Puerto Rico was declared for the first
time. The rich history of The Nationalist Party and its leader
Pedro Albizu Campos, the Malcolm X of Puerto Rico. Albizu
was educated at Harvard in the 1930s and ended up advocat-
ing armed resistance against the United States, which controlled
the government, the military, and the economy. And that control continued to this day, I learned. Communications, curren-
cy, trade, citizenship/naturalization, labor relations, banking
systems, Social Security, unemployment and disability bene-

fits, environmental laws—all this and more were dictated by the United States Congress. The FBI ran internal security. The CIA took care of the rest.

Taking Puerto Rican studies at Hunter College also resulted in a renewed determination to speak Spanish more often, to become more fluent. Since struggling through the advanced Spanish-language courses back at Cardinal Hayes High School, I never sought to brush up on my native tongue. Not that I'd ever come close to forgetting it: I just didn't practice it enough. I began listening to Salsa music virtually every day, and traded in my flower shirts, which I still wore a lot, for *guayaberas* and a T-shirt saying *¡Que Viva Puerto Rico Libre!*

Milton was thrilled that I was now an *independentista*.

"Now you can be on the FBI's Most Wanted List."

"*¡Que viva!*"

"I wish I could've gone to college."

"You still could, Milton. There isn't an age limit to an education."

"I get it right here. The Mailroom University."

That was certainly true. Everybody who worked in the SSC&B mailroom, as well as those who visited it for business or pleasure, got a whiff of politics, which wound its way into discussions about everything from movies to current events. An ad executive once told Milton: "I don't care what you think. *Gone With The Wind* was a great movie." To which Milton replied:

"The only great part of the movie was the burning of Atlanta."

Milton had to deal with the fact that he was a supervisor. One of the mailroom workers, Little Tito, asked him, "If bosses are bad, then what about you?"

"I'm a supervisor."

"That's what I'm saying. You're a good boss."

"I'm not a boss."

"But—"

"I'm not a capitalist either. Do you see me investing in machinery, owning a bank, expanding into other countries? Am I like the rich execs upstairs?"

"No, but you want to be."

Despite the political goings on in the mailroom, we had more than our fair share of backward comments and behavior. Guys tossed around the usual amount of antigay remarks. "Hey, that's a nice shirt. Do they make it for men?" was a favorite. Juan, a mailroom lifer from Uruguay, who was openly gay, would retaliate by grabbing his balls and saying, "You want some of this?"

Notwithstanding the warts, we prided ourselves in the importance of our work, how central it was to keep the operations afloat. It nurtured individual pride too. It was common for others in the company to call us "mail boys." This became less prevalent over the years as we *never* let that go. "How old do I have to be before you stop calling me a boy?

CHAPTER SEVENTEEN

etween Hunter College and the Mailroom University, I
was now getting some much-needed brain food. It wasn't
so much to be thinking deeply again. It was thinking in a new
way, as if I was mining hidden treasures, including within myself. I read *The Communist Manifesto* again because I really
wanted to understand it. It seemed "out there" in a way, and that
added to its appeal, like the authors were challenging me. And
they were young when they wrote the book. Marx was thir-
ty-two. Engels was twenty-eight. *What will I be doing when I
was twenty-eight?*

At work one late August afternoon, Milton handed me a
flyer.

"Conference of Workers World Party?" I said.

Milton said he had run into them at a protest against subway and bus fare hikes, where they were chanting, "The subways
should be free!" Afterward, he and members of Workers World
had gotten into some "deep discussions," and they invited him
to their two-day Labor Day Conference.

"They told me to bring friends. Want to go?"

"If they're for free subways, sure, why not?" I said.

The 1976 National Conference of Workers World Party
(WWP) took place at the Marc Ballroom in Union Square in

Manhattan, a fancy place to house a communist gathering, I thought. After registering at a table staffed by a rather ebullient young woman, I entered the carpeted hall. A couple of hundred people were there, maybe more. Although whites predominated, the crowd was a mix of nationalities and age groups, from teenagers to senior citizens. Nametags told me that people came from Norfolk, Cleveland, Baltimore, Detroit, San Francisco, and dozens of other cities. A few had traveled from abroad, including Africa, the Middle East and Latin America.

There was a lot of literature. And posters. And banners on the wall with exclamation marks. WWP seemed to cover just about every base imaginable, from trade-union struggles and the plight of undocumented immigrants to slogans proclaiming, "Only Socialist Revolution Can End Racism & Imperialist War!"

I scooped up several tons of leaflets and handouts and found Milton sitting at a round table with a few people. He got up and gave me a bear hug. "You made it, *compañero!*" he said.

"I told you I'd be here. Man, this is something."

One of the guys at the table leaned over and looked at my nametag. "Welcome, David Perez from the South Bronx!"

"Is this your first time here?" an elderly woman asked.

"Yes, it is.

"It won't be your last!"

"Friendly blokes," I whispered to Milton.

"And militant."

"That too."

The opening plenary featured Sam Marcy, the Workers World Party chairman. He stood five foot three, give or take, a Jewish man in his 50s with thick eyebrows, big ears, and a luminous smile. He reminded me of a deli owner. Sam began his speech acknowledging Vietnam, which in July had officially declared itself "The Socialist Republic of Vietnam." Thunderous applause greeted a three-person delegation from the newly united nation, their slight heights topped with golden brown faces that exuded strength and pride. These are the people who defeated the U.S. military, I thought to myself, and they're barely taller than my mother.

Sam Marcy next described how U.S. banks and the International Monetary Fund were taking over the Polish economy. What the banking elite wanted with Poland, Sam said, was to dismantle its "socialist-oriented" economy and break its alliance with the Soviet Union. "Not for the benefit of the Polish people," he said, "But because finance capital needs to expand its domination of the globe."

I scratched my head and poked Milton. "Why is he talking about Poland?"

"It's important."

"Poland?"

"Just listen."

Sam then linked what was happening with Poland to what banks did to people in the United States, using the lure of loans to lasso individuals and communities into an ever-tightening knot of debt and dependency. I scratched my head again. Guess I gotta read more.

I'm not sure how he arrived at the U.S. prison system, but once there, Sam explained how prisons were "concentration camps for the poor." How the rich never go to jail because they owned the system that produced them. This got Sam riled.

"People accuse us of wanting to tear down the prison walls," he said, tugging on a keychain. "Well, that's exactly what we want to do!"

Prolonged applause. I clapped too, thinking this was the most radical stuff I'd ever heard. Tear down the prisons? *Let everyone out?*

Sam then saluted the Black youth of Soweto in South Africa, who had risen up en masse against apartheid, and whose struggle was intimately tied to that of Black America, which itself was "part and parcel of the global struggle against U.S. imperialism." Ditto the struggle for Puerto Rico's independence (at which point I raised my fist and yelled, "*¡Que Viva!*").

Sam finished his two-hour speech, given entirely without notes, declaring that "poor and working people" all over the world were perfectly capable of running society themselves.

"And one day we will do so! Victory to the Socialist Revolution!"

Standing ovation. I stood and applauded too, blown away by Sam's connect-the-dots talk. Some of it seemed a stretch, but somehow he managed to pull it off, a tour de force of intellect. It jarred me. If I had seen Sam Marcy in the street, I'd think him an average Joe, with his nondescript buttoned shirt, simple slacks and sensible shoes—not the least bit threatening. Yet he'd fired off a speech that called for revolution and letting the inmates loose.

I turned to the elderly woman next to me. "That little white dude is *bad.*"

She grinned. "Fucking A!"

The rest of the two-day conference was filled with dozens of talks on issues too numerous to name, all given by everyday people: union workers from Buffalo, welfare mothers from Atlanta, students from Chicago. Besides the talks, I picked up tidbits of WWP's program through photos and discussions with various people, how they supported all struggles for social justice but identified most closely with groups like the Young Lords and Black Panthers, with Trotsky as opposed to Stalin. They supported the Chinese Revolution. They supported every anticolonial movement known to humankind. Strangely, nothing I heard sounded rhetorical or overly strident. Well, maybe a little.

They had an impressive list of firsts too. In 1962 their youth wing, Youth Against War and Fascism, organized the first picket line protesting U.S. involvement in Vietnam. Ho Chi Minh publicly saluted the activity in a letter to *The New York Times*. Again, this was in 1962, years before the war officially began. During the Vietnam War, party members also started the American Servicemen's Union, whose newspaper, *The Bond*, was the first antiwar newspaper put out by rank-and-file GIs.

One interesting factoid I picked up was that even Albert Einstein thought highly of socialism. In 1948, he wrote an essay in the journal *Monthly Review* that denounced "the economic anarchy" and "crippling egotism" of capitalist society and called for "the establishment of a socialist economy, accompanied by an educational system oriented toward social goals."

Who knew?

***

Walking home after the conference—which ended in a series of chants and the singing of the Internationale, a stirring song that made me feel kind of hokey—my brain was churning on overdrive. Milton was euphoric and said he was definitely joining Workers World.

"What about you?" he asked.

"I want to think about it. I know what you're going to say. 'What's to think about?' I just need to work it through my system, let it percolate."

"What's to percolate?"

"I'm not really sure."

In my miniature apartment on Fourth Street and Avenue A, I made myself a rum and Coke and plopped down on my well-traveled sofa. I considered smoking a joint but decided against it. I still partook in getting high. Nowhere near the volume I used to do, but I still enjoyed a good head.

It was close to midnight and the streets outside were noisy. The Lower East Side, aka Alphabet City, was a true melting pot of cultures. Twenty languages could be heard on one block. Around the corner was a Ukrainian pastry shop, a Chinese-owned dry cleaners, a Cuban restaurant, and a deli owned by a Polish family. I wondered what they thought about what U.S. banks were doing to their country?

I refilled my drink. When Milton said he was joining Workers World, my immediate instinct was to say, "Me too!" But I was glad I didn't. I did want to let it percolate. Too many times my decisions in life had been rash, thoughtless, a pinball machine constantly hitting tilt. Yet my life felt like it had finally settled down. I was learning to be a father. I had a nice job and was connecting my own dots.

Closing my eyes, my mind floated to my Honors class at Cardinal Hayes, when I first recognized—albeit in a hard-to-define way—that I felt comfortable being among various nationalities. The same held true at Aviation, whose student body was thoroughly multinational. Then there was the Navy, another sea of nationalities. I thought back to the conversation with Miss Collins, the counselor at Miramar. She had asked me where exactly I thought I belonged, the same question I'd often asked myself.

I sipped my drink. More dots came together. Many things had stood out for me at the Workers World Party conference, strongest among them a feeling of belonging and connecting to something beyond myself, beyond community and country. Repeatedly, I'd heard the word "internationalism." Could the reason I couldn't nail exactly where I belonged be that I simply belonged everywhere?

Internationalism. Yes, that was it.

CHAPTER EIGHTEEN

A few months later, in early 1977, I joined Workers World Party. Thus began what would turn into fifteen years of me "in the movement," when I became in word and in a deed a citizen of the world.

On the one hand, my pride in being a Puerto Rican revolutionary became firmly rooted. At the same time, I embraced being part of the global working class, a class with the power to run society for need and not for profit. Utopian? A dream? At times, it felt exactly like that. But what's worth fighting for if not our dreams? I was taught in Catholic school that the "meek shall inherit the earth." What if that were true? What if, as an addendum, we weren't meek at all?

My knowledge of the world grew immeasurably. I knew about East Harlem, but what about East Timor? Workers World organized a small demonstration (fewer than 40 people) calling for the country's freedom from U.S.-backed Indonesian rule.[2] At a coffee shop, I chatted with Jose Horta Ramos, then a representative of the popular movement and later the first president of East Timor. To me, he was a regular guy, chatting politics over a cup of Joe.

Not lasting long enough in the Navy to visit other lands,

2 The history of East Timor is better known these days, but not back in 1979. This was another example of WWP being ahead of the curve on political issues.

the lands came to me. I met activists and leaders from Chile, El Salvador, Palestine, South Africa, Mexico, Jamaica, Argentina, and Korea, to name a few. It seemed like the entire world had a gripe against the U.S. government, and it's banking and corporate elite. At times, it felt like my head would explode trying to keep up with all the various struggles raging over the earth. But mostly it felt cool.

Milton Vera and me at a WWP demonstration in 1980

Moreover, I learned to think not only in global terms but also in class terms, to view issues from the prism of how it affected poor and working people, that there were sides to a struggle, even if that side was multifaceted.

What especially inspired me was learning the stories of the

people who lived and worked in the United States, as told by labor unions, Black and Latino people, the voices of the voiceless and the downtrodden. These were the type of people I had grown up with in the Millbrook projects and at school, the guys I hung out with in the Navy, the guys working in the mailroom, my family. There's a pride in being *obrero*, in belonging to a multi-colored, multi-generational working class, whose labor truly makes the world go round, as just one general strike in one country can attest. If being a communist taught me only that, it would be worth everything.

It was like being prescribed a pair of class glasses. Beforehand, I would see a strike of sanitation workers strictly from the view of personal inconvenience, and I would essentially parrot the media view that these workers were selfish and overpaid. Now I hailed the power of the sanitation workers and recognized just how vital their work was, so much so that they could never be overpaid. The problem isn't that they make "good money." The problem is that all workers should make good money, including all of us in the mailroom.

Class glasses. Everybody should own a pair.

***

Part of becoming more hip to the power of labor was mining the field of political economy. For most of my life, economics just didn't feel relevant to anything, even as I knew, as did most people, that "Money talks and bullshit walks." That saying doesn't seem profound but, in a way, it said it all. But who gets all the money? And how do they get it?

I'll never forget how Vince Copeland, a former steelworker, stage actor, and one of the founding members of Workers World, a man both brilliant and down to earth, laid it out.

"The main thing you should know about the dollar is that you haven't got any," Vince explained to me. "Every day in the papers you see stories about millions and billions of dollars, about mergers of big corporations, about so many billions for the banks. That's the dollar, the one they're always trying to save.

"Their dollar."

"Exactly. You don't even see the dollar except on paydays and soon you're plumb out of dollars again. What happened to the dollars? You paid them to the landlord, the supermarket, the electric company and other billionaire corporations. Maybe you put a few dollars in the bank. The banks then take your dollars—"

"And other people's dollars," I added.

"And other people's dollars. And then they lend them to some corporation, with interest, that then hires other workers to sweat for their dollars and they in turn recycle it in the system and on it goes. The dollar has become capital."

"And all I get in return is my shirt."

"And probably not a very good one."

***

Another aspect of my new life that got resolved in this period was my longtime defensiveness over being school smart, which was rarely as important as being street smart, tough smart, "bad mother" smart. Now I felt all the above. After my high school graduation, Milton had reminded me that there were different types of smart, and that people could be one or more. I agreed. But inside, there remained something extra special about being the street kind. That added a whole other dimension.

Take Malcolm X. He was a hustler and thief who became a revolutionary leader of the highest intellect, a man of color who "talked the talk and walked the walk." In the hood, there was no higher compliment.

What made Malcolm so extraordinary was his understanding of the street, of the brothers in the joint. In jail, he studied the dictionary and then elevated the talk and became an incredible orator and writer. But he still spoke both languages.

Of course, I was far from being a Malcolm, and I wouldn't pretend otherwise. But I did straddle both worlds. In general, the guys from the block dug it when I gave out issues of *Workers World*, railed against capitalism, and rapped about how Che Guevara was the "baddest mother" ever.

Some of the fellas thought I'd flipped. One day, Jaime, a fellow member of WWP, related to me what he'd overheard in the gym.

"The other day I was in the locker room at the YMCA, getting dressed, and I hear these guys talking in the row of lockers behind mine. One of them says, 'Yo, remember David Perez from the Millbrook projects?' The other guy said yeah, and the first guy says that David is 'like a Communist and shit now' and the second dude can't believe it."

"They actually said that? In those words?" I asked.

"That's an exact quote. Then they started to laugh, and one of them said, 'David was always into something.' And the other guy called you Brainiac."

Those were definitely friends from the block! They were the only ones who called me Brainiac, my nickname from St. Luke's Elementary School. Jaime never found out who they were, though.

***

Besides Milton and me, the only person from our neighborhood who joined Workers World Party was Raphael Ramos, the first person to talk to me about needing to "get down with the people's struggle" back in 1969. Raphael, or Ray as we mostly called him, had struggled for years with heroin addiction but was on a clean streak when Milton and I began talking with him about WWP. What nailed his decision to join was a 1979 demonstration in Buffalo, New York, protesting the Ku Klux Klan's plan to march on Martin Luther King Jr.'s birthday. WWP vowed not to let that happen. At the demo, we put sticks inside the hollow banner poles and padded our arms with thick foam with cardboard linings, ready to ward off any attacks.

Ray was impressed. "Damn, these are some serious dudes. Ready to rumble."

"That's why I'm here," I said, cracking my knuckles.

The KKK never materialized, much to my relief.

I loved having Ray around. He was what one would politely call blunt. Refreshingly so. One time we were at a protest, and this anally cerebral dude was riding Ray about how "real Marxists" needed to understand all the intricacies of philosophy and political economy and how it was all "so terribly complicated" and so on and so forth until Ray finally said: "I got something Marxist for you. Shut the fuck up."

Another guy from the block who eventually came around was Big Danny. As a young teenager, he and I never really hung together, except for smoking pot a couple of times in the Big Park, but that was always in a group. Danny was an amateur boxer and a skilled trainer who honed his trade with the Social Seven, the neighborhood gang back in the day when gangs didn't wear colors and earned respect on pure rep. Danny was also the guy who ended up with my first girlfriend, Carmen, the girl I dated and never kissed.

Actually, it was at the SSC&B mailroom that we won over Danny. He worked for the firm's maintenance department, which, like the mailroom, was part of Office Services. Danny would occasionally come into the mailroom brandishing his

Dewitt Clinton High School history textbook to show Milton and me how we had it all wrong.

"See this? It says we live in a free country!" he'd say.

"Only if you can afford it," I'd counter.

"At least I can say it."

"Say what?"

"That we live in a free country!"

And then Danny would crack up like he didn't really buy what he was saying, like he was just testing us. Danny had razor-sharp wit and an innate sense of right and wrong. He also knew a lot about indigenous people's history, much more than I did. With that came his knowledge of the genocide perpetrated on Native Americans by the U.S. government, and who this "free country" really belonged to—not to mention what used to belong to Mexico.

After going to several meetings and demonstrations, Danny became a "friend" of Workers World, who had tons of official friends way before Facebook. Danny never joined, which suited me fine. It was great just having him around, another link to the old neighborhood chain. Plus he never stopped asking tough questions, which kept me on my toes.

At one point, Ray also got a job in the mailroom, and with him on board, and Danny dropping in every day, the mailroom became a recruitment office as we bombarded every messenger and visitor with a dose of Marxism, an issue of *Workers World*, and plenty of heated arguments. Some people were won over; most were not. But, man, we were on all the time. As the head of Personnel once remarked, "Whenever I visit the mailroom, I get an education and a half."

But sometimes we were the ones who got schooled.

CHAPTER NINETEEN

"**O**kay, guys, listen up," Milton says. "We're going to be in a company video that's going to be shown at the Christmas Party."

"Like in a movie?" Crazy Mikey asks.

"Yeah. Nick from the Creative Department just called me and asked when he could come shoot. I told him to show up this afternoon."

At three PM, Nick arrives with a colleague lugging a film camera, the kind used by TV crews. Nick's a hyper-enthusiastic Italian American with pointy ears. His department created all the jingles and copy for TV and radio commercials and for print ads. Nick thought it cool to shoot a short movie about the company and show it at the Christmas Party. He wants it to be funny and clever and inclusive.

"Okay here's the setup," Nick says, breathlessly. "There's going to be a phone ringing and you all are going to respond by, get this, *not doing anything*. That's right. You can remain standing, be taking a nap, whatever. Basically, you'll just ignore the ring. It'll be a smash!"

"What about my wardrobe?" Crazy Mikey asks.

"Don't worry about it," Little Tito says. "That's a nice shirt, do they make it for men?"

"Right here!" Juan says, grabbing his balls.

Milton shakes his head.

"Okay, get into a position," Nick says.

"I need makeup," says Little Tito.

"You need this!" Juan yells, hand still on nuts.

We scurry into position. Little Tito mounts a counter and curls up in a fetal position. Crazy Mikey sprawls himself on the floor like a crime victim. Ray lights up a cigarette and makes smoke rings. Juan stands frozen like a statue. I pretend to be dozing face down on the desk.

Nick stares at us. "I love it!"

Milton says he wants to be reading a newspaper and takes out an issue of *Workers World*, red star on its masthead proclaiming "Workers and Oppressed of the World Unite!".

Nick strokes his mustache "I don't know. It's a bit risqué but… brilliant! I love it!"

The cameraman whispers in Nick's ear. He nods.

"Capital idea! Milton, we'll have the camera open on you as the phone rings. I want you to ever so slowly slide the paper down as you 'hear' the phone ringing. Then you'll ever so slowly pull it back in front of your face. After that Sal will pan the room at everyone else who's not responding. Got it? Good, everyone back into positions!"

We do as instructed. I glance over at Milton, holding his communist newspaper. *Are you freaking kidding me?*

"And action!"

The camera stays on Milton as he inches the paper ever so slowly down and then back up, his face stoic. Sal the camera-man sweeps the room on the rest of us.

"Cut!" Nick yells. He pauses to stroke his mustache. "Okay, you're all naturals, but this time I want you to *really imagine the phone ringing*."

"Like it's *really* ringing?" Crazy Mikey asks.

"Exactly."

We nod and basically do the exact same thing. I lament my choice to be face down. I won't be seen!

"Cut, that's a print!" Our wannabe director gushes and Sal gives us a thumbs-up. We all shake hands, and they leave.

Little Tito is slapping everyone five, "Our first movie!"

"And you're not even getting paid, you dumb fuck," Ray says.

I go over to Milton, who's grinning like he'd won a round of poker. "You're crazy with the *Workers World*."

"Yeah. Imagine if they use it?"

The Holiday Party happens a week later. SSC&B had a banner year and rented out a banquet hall in a plush midtown hotel replete with chandeliers, huge buffet tables, and enough beer, wine and spirits to fill the Hudson River. We didn't have Caligula at the bash, but he would have felt right at home—sec-retaries on the prowl without their husbands, and a few with them in tow. A few affairs and steamy one-night stands will undoubtedly be hatched this evening, as they have in years past.

Once again, the guys in the mailroom are the stars of the show. There's some self-serving in this, of course. A dash of "as if!" But it's largely true. We were the street guys, young mostly, who knew how to dance and how to party: Salsa, Disco, Motown, you name it. If a country tune came on we became Freddy Fender. With oldies we morphed into Chubby Checker. This year is no exception.

After a couple of hours of over-the-top dancing and gyrating, somebody blows a whistle. It's Nick, microphone in hand, sauced like everyone else. Sal is next to him wearing a Santa hat and a Hawaiian necklace.

"Okay, it's time for our, ahem, surprise movie!" Nick yells amid hoots and cheers. "It's a smash!"

I join my fellow mailroom crew. Big Danny comes over. "Is this where Milton is reading *Workers World?*" he asks.

"We'll see," I say.

"I hope the feds aren't here," Danny says.

A screen appears and everyone quiets down. Nick had made the movie as a parody centering on the CEO needing a "new and hot" advertising slogan to win an important client. The narration is to the tune of "The Night Before Christmas," rather clever. Halfway through the video, the CEO telephones for help, including the mailroom. And there we are: phone ringing as a copy of *Workers World* with its red banner slides ever so slowly down, revealing the stony face of Milton.

I clap him on the back. "I can't believe it. You pulled it off."

"You just gotta be bold," he says.

Danny looks around for the feds. "All clear."

Measured chuckles have filled the banquet hall, room, which quickly turns into roaring laughter as the camera pans to the rest of us. Little Tito gets the most laughs for his fetal position. I sigh at seeing only the top of my head. At least my Shag looks neat.

The video continues. The CEO is scratching his head, frustrated over the inability of such a talented company to create a winning campaign. Oh dear, oh dear. Just when all hope is gone, into his office comes the head maintenance man, Herman, saying, "What's happening!" in his thick Spanish accent. Everybody in the holiday party howls, the laughter reaching a crescendo when Herman saves the day by figuring out the perfect jungle.

Ray is tight-lipped. "Isn't that the funniest thing you've ever seen?" he says. "Imagine that, a Puerto Rican janitor being so smart."

CHAPTER TWENTY

I christened Milton, Ray, Danny, and myself the "Gang of Four." Being the eldest by a few years, Milton was the "Grand Papa," a moniker he reveled in and earned, reveled because it made him sort of a sage, dolling out Marxist phrases fortune cookie style. Earned because Milton a) got most of us jobs, and b) lent us money by licking his fingers and peeling off dollar bills from a rolled up wad of money the size of an apple.

Our gang's calling card was our long walks. They usually began after attending a Workers World meeting at its meeting hall on 12th Street and University Avenue in downtown Manhattan, after which we'd walk for miles on end.

Alongside our marathon walks were our marathon talks, which covered vast expanses of territory: the wit and wisdom of Leon Trotsky; Fidel Castro's courage and intellect; the choices oppressed people had between success and survival, revolution and despair; how everything in our lives were linked, a labyrinth getting resolved and then entangled again, a synthesis of growing up in the streets and dreaming of the stars.

We talked about raising kids and our love lives, or lack of them. About whether the Third World was really the First World, because after all, weren't we here first? About our Taíno ancestors, and those who came before them, who had lived and prospered eons before Columbus and imperialism arrived and "fucked things up," as Ray aptly put it.

Anchoring our conversations was "the block," an entity all its own. The block served as final judge and jury, the ultimate arbiter. "Try talking that shit around the block!" or "Wait till the block hears about this!"

***

One memorable summer evening, our Gang of Four walked all the way to the block, a distance of fifteen miles. We started at 10 p.m. and finished at two in the morning, making a few pit stops along the way.

When we got to the East 50's, we began snapping on what happened at this apartment I used to live in at 53rd Street and Second Avenue, not too far from the job. The rent was $235 a month and it took having a roommate for me to pay it. I threw some great parties there, though, with enough pot to level several elephants.

For some unfathomable reason, I once invited two guys from Workers World who were disdainful of drugs. Before they arrived, I became frantic and told people to put away the marijuana. They laughed and blew smoke in my eye. When the uptight duo arrived, they inhaled and frowned. Leaving their coats on, they refused my offer of Cheese Doodles and left.

"That was so funny," Danny said.

"We should never forget how drugs are killing our community," Milton said.

"But is pot a drug?" I countered.

"For now yeah." Milton didn't get high, but he loved his liquor. He wasn't a lush by any means. But he could belt a few.

Ray was quiet. He had long struggled with the needle, having been in drug rehab twice, including one that preached the "Word of Christ" to get you clean.

Drugs had always been a dicey, complex issue for us. On one end, we knew plenty of people who fought the good fight and still enjoyed a joint or two. But the issue was loaded for Black and Latin people. The three-strikes-you're-out Rockefeller laws had skyrocketed the prison population, mostly with Black and brown faces. The war on drugs was really a war on us.

"Should we stop here?" Danny asked.

"No, let's keep walking," I said.

We got to 100th Street and Lexington Ave, which Ray called "the ghetto line."

"One block north and we're in El Barrio. One block south and we're back with the rich *blanquitos*," he said.

White people were yet another layered topic. The four of us shared a pride in our roots, but we'd become of citizens of the world, clearly recognizing the issue of race but using our "class glasses" to go beyond it. We'd also become more conscious of women's oppression, of the struggle of lesbian and gay people. Nonetheless, there invariably remained the *blanquito*, an indefinable yet crystal clear mode of being.

"Should we stop here?" I asked.

"No, let's keep going," Ray said.

We walked through East Harlem, crossed the Willis Avenue Bridge, made our way past Chichamba—which evoked more memories of times good and bad—and arrived in the Big Park. The evening was warm and smog hid the stars. We sat on a bench and stretched our legs.

It struck me as fitting that we were in the Big Park. When I graduated from St. Luke's in 1969, my friends and I celebrated the milestone right on the very bench I was sitting in now, sipping Colt 45, having my first puff of a Kool cigarette. The bench was where Chino waxed lovingly about cutting class, getting high, and doing "The Grind" at hooky gigs, sealing my fate. Everything happened here: The Big Park, the Grand Central Station of the Millbrook Houses.

"No matter what, this always feels like home," I said. "Remember when President Carter made his visit to the South Bronx, looking all shocked at the burnt-out buildings and rubble?"

"That was Charlotte Street, around 170th Street, up past Hunts Point," Milton said.

"What made me do a double take was that when we grew up, Charlotte Street was not the South Bronx. The South Bronx began on 132nd Street and ended on 149th Street. That was it!"

"Maybe we should call this the Deep South," Big Danny said.

"It's like when the poverty and arson spread so did the geography," I continued. "To me, we're the *real* South Bronx, you know what I mean?"

"Fucking A," Ray said. "That was a good talk you gave, David."

At the meeting we'd come from, I had given an "educational" on undocumented workers, explaining how there should be no borders in our struggle as workers. "After all, capital roams freely from country to country" I'd said. "No visas required, no border patrols to arrest you. Why should it be different with labor?"

I had become a good public speaker. Who knew? The first time I spoke at a Party meeting, I couldn't even look up from the microphone. I stuttered and sweated as if I'd just run a cross-country race. But Workers World was a great training ground. If you had an untapped talent, an unknown gift, you learned how to develop it. Mine, it turned out, was being able to engage and educate an audience.

I'd also awakened a long dormant muse by writing weekly articles for *Workers World* newspaper. Up to then, the only story I had ever written, or at least that I had enjoyed writing, was "As the City Sleeps," my tribute, as it were, to my South Bronx buddies and the dangers of the thug life. Now I was being given assignments like covering a demonstration about saving a healthcare clinic or a protest against police brutality. This was partisan reporting to the nth degree, activist journalism that

proudly took a side. I wasn't trying to be "objective," which I
came to think was largely a bullshit term. How can one not take
sides in a world divided by sides?

"I wonder if I'll ever want to move back here," I said. "How
about you guys? Ever miss living in the block?"

"Sometimes," Danny said.

"It's living inside us," Ray added. "We never really left."

"Yeah, we'll always be ghetto," said Milton. "But in a good
way."

"If we go the right way, we'll never go the wrong way," I said.

They looked at me and laughed.

"Is that like your new philosophy?" Ray asked.

"It's something my father likes to say. It's funny. He always
says it to me as if it just popped into his head, like it's the key
to life."

"Maybe it is," Milton said.

I laughed. Yeah, maybe it is.

Preview of WOW! 3:
Who You Gonna Believe?

"Forty is an age of new beginnings," Veronica told me the night of my birthday. "Maybe you need a new adventure."

I sighed and gallantly took a bite of my Boca Burger, a meatless patty. Forty was also a time for a new diet, Veronica had insisted. Much as I wanted to enjoy it, the Boca just didn't cut the mustard, so to speak, even with a stack of fried organic purple onions heaped on top of it. Veronica poured me a glass of freshly squeezed carrot juice, courtesy of our recently purchased space age blender, and we toasted our mutual commitment to better health and saving the planet.

The year was 1995, and I had spent the last twenty years enmeshed in the radical political movement. Despite the collapse of the Soviet Union, despite the loudly trumpeted "triumph of capitalism," I considered myself an unrepentant leftist. Still, age does something to you. Notwithstanding my convictions, I was hungry for... something else.

"Funny that you should mention adventure; I'm thinking I might check this out," I said and handed Veronica a catalog advertising "The New Life Expo," a two-day symposium on natural health, spirituality and the paranormal. The event, scheduled for the coming weekend at the Roosevelt Hotel in midtown Manhattan, promised "hundreds of speakers and exhibits."

"Hey, it's organized by *New Life* magazine," Veronica said. "Kind of appropriate, don't you think?"

"There's also a guy who'll be talking about *past lives*. That should be a hoot."

"One life is plenty for me."

"But what I really want to hear is this lecture by someone called Reverend Petersen about 'Aliens, Angels, and the Pleiades.' That's a star system."

"A Reverend?"

"That's what the program says."

"I get the angels part, but aliens? Little green men?"

"They might not be green."

"Well—"

"And we're getting all green anyway. So it's all linked. Sort of. I used to gobble this paranormal stuff up as a kid. My brother George and I were super deep into comic books, especially Marvel: *The Incredible Hulk, The Fantastic Four, The Uncanny X-Men.*"

"Big adjectives."

"We actually learned to speak English that way, reading comics. That and TV. When you think about it, comic books have pretty sophisticated dialogue: descriptions of intergalactic empires and futuristic weaponry. Anyway, I was about ten years old, third grade at P.S. 65, when I ordered this book called

Amazing Tales—or something like that—from the Scholastic Book Club for Kids. It was one of those 'amazing but true' collections."

"Another adjective."

"Two stories I remember to this day. The first was about this London watchman guarding a warehouse in a pier. Inside were a bunch of caskets to be shipped somewhere. Being London, the evening was foggy. All of a sudden, a tremor shakes the pier and knocks the guard off his feet. He picks himself up and goes inside the warehouse to check the cargo. Guess what he found?"

"I can't."

"The coffins were open—with all the bodies gone!"

"Want some celery?"

Author's Note

As with my first "memoirito," WOW! (11B Press, 2011), I've combined some characters and changed the names of others. Chronologically, events occurred pretty much in the order presented. Memory is often selective and hazy, and I'm certain others will remember some of this story differently. But I've done my best to tell the truth, and memory always has its own story to tell.

About the Author

Author, actor, and teacher David Pérez loves to create and share stories from the page to the stage. He is the founder of Verdad Creative, which offers a wide range of public performance, writing and editing services (verdadcreative.com). He lives in Taos, NM with his wife, poet Veronica Golos.

www.ingramcontent.com/pod-product-compliance
Lightning Source LLC
Chambersburg PA
CBHW032037040426
42449CB00007B/917